This Belongs To :--
Anita L. Schachtel
22 Ketchum Place
Buffalo, New York.

ISRAEL IN CANAAN

CANAAN
THE PROMISED LAND
BEFORE THE CONQUEST

FERTILE REGION

SNOW CAPPED MT. HERMON

CARAVAN FROM DAMASCUS

WOODED HILLS

CEDARS OF LEBANON

RIVER YARMUK

GILEAD
WHERE GROW THE HEALING HERBS

RIVER JABBOK

GALILEE

CHINNERETH

JORDAN

RIVER KISHON

PLAIN OF JEZREEL

HIGH FERTILE PLATEAU

MT. CARMEL

SAND DUNES

MARSH LAND

GREAT SEA OR SEA OF THE

RICH PASTURE LANDS

RIVER ARNON

GREAT PLATEAU

MT. NEBO

N

SCALE OF MILES
0   5   10   20   30

DATE PALMS

JERICHO

THRESHING BARLEY

JERUSALEM

SALT SEA
(DEAD SEA)

MUD HUTS

CAVE DWELLINGS

VINE COVERED TERRACES

HERD OF GOATS

ENTRANCE TO PETRA

COASTAL PLAIN

RICH FRUIT TREES

CARAVAN ROUTE TO EGYPT

SHEPHELA OR LOWLAND

RICH FIELDS of WHEAT AND CORN

NEGEB OR SOUTH COUNTRY

KADESH-BARNEA

32

31

36

35

31

32

ISRAEL IN CANAAN

By JACOB S. GOLUB, Ph.D.

Author of *In the Days of the
Second Temple*

CINCINNATI

Department of Synagogue and School Extension
of the Union of American Hebrew Congregations

1930

TO

LEO AND HULDAH

AND TO

ALL THEIR CONTEMPORARIES

THIS VOLUME

IS LOVINGLY DEDICATED

Editor's Introduction

The kind reception given by rabbis, teachers and principals to "In the Days of the Second Temple" by Dr. Jacob S. Golub when this book first made its appearance in the spring of 1929, proved conclusively that it fulfilled a genuinely felt need.

"Israel in Canaan," which the Department of Synagogue and School Extension takes pleasure in presenting to Jewish schools, was prepared by the same author, whose training and experience in Jewish education have eminently fitted him for the task of writing history for young people.

Until now the Jewish teacher in search of a text book on the biblical period had to choose one of the many versions of Bible stories or one of the biblical histories written by non-Jews. The former did not introduce the child to Jewish history at all; the latter too often proved unsatisfactory from a Jewish point of view.

The present volume differs from both of these. It does not retell the Bible stories; it treats biblical history with a view to presenting the gradual development of the Jewish people from small beginnings until it became a nation. It reflects, at the same

ix

time, the attitude of one who is steeped in Jewish life, and who therefore sees constant interrelations between the past of his people and their present problems.

This volume, as the previous one, is the result of years of teaching and experimentation. Hence, it is not merely a history, but a "new Jewish history based on sound pedagogic theory and deeply rooted in experience with children." Once more the problem approach has been used, and each chapter represents a selection and organization of material which should be of help to the teacher who appreciates the function which the problem performs in stimulating thought and wholesome activity. The material of ancient history becomes vital, and assumes new life.

Unlike most text books of this period which stress names, dates, and political events, this book gives emphasis to the development of the social life of the early Hebrews, thus laying the foundation for an intelligent understanding and appreciation of later Jewish religious ideals.

In order to adjust the classroom instruction to the individual needs of the more capable pupils, some thought questions have been appended to each section. Projects including map work have been arranged, and an adequate bibliography for each section has been added for pupil and teacher. Readings from the Bible, and particularly from the series of Bible readers especially prepared for children by the Department of Synagogue and School Extension, have been selected in order to acquaint the children with the most important source for biblical history, as well as with the use of source material in general. In addition, the Department of Synagogue and School Extension has spared no effort to make the appearance of the book attractive as far as type, illustrations, maps, time lines and cover are concerned.

The Editor is confident that once again, the Department of Synagogue and School Extension is presenting to the children of our Jewish schools a text book which represents a new writing of biblical history from a Jewish point of view, which will help our children to an intelligent understanding of their own inspiring past, and which will give them hope for the future of their people.

EMANUEL GAMORAN.

Preface

THE writer feels called upon to begin this volume with a word of explanation. It may seem somewhat out of logical order that a text treating of the beginnings of our history should appear after a book has been prepared dealing with the period of the days of the Second Temple. Further, the author can hardly claim the distinction of having issued a new volume within a year and a half after the earlier text. The present book, *Israel in Canaan*, with its companion volume, *In the Days of the First Temple*, which will appear shortly, were actually begun about eight or nine years ago. After the work was more than half finished, it was laid aside at the request of Dr. Gamoran, who urged the need of a volume to cover the period of the Second Temple. That book being completed, the earlier work was resumed, and brought down to the year 586 B.C.E.

As in the preface to his previous volume, the writer wishes to repeat that he is not a professional historian and particularly senses his inadequacy in attempting to thread his way through the many conflicting theories concerning our early history. If the present volume is any contribution at all, it is mainly in selection of material and in method of treatment. The main criterion which the writer has set before himself has been to show the beginning of our people as a natural unfolding, influenced by all the factors which shape social groups everywhere. If we are to look forward to a Jewish future and shall not merely rest upon our past, it is essential that we recognize Israel's genius as evidenced in continuous and recurring growth rather than in a once-for-all bloom after which we have merely followed a fixed pattern.

There is generally misunderstanding about the age group for which a given volume is intended. This text has been written for normal use in the seventh grade, but has been tested and simplified so that it can also serve in the sixth.

Sufficient supplementary exercises in the form of thought questions, map exercises and Bible study have been provided to meet individual differences among pupils who will use this text. The writer did not wish to enlarge upon his study aids because of the very excellent pupil's work book which has been substantially completed by Mr. Edward Nudelman of the Board of Jewish Education of Chicago. There is therefore no need of duplicating the work here and teachers who would avail themselves of such assistance and suggestions are urged to familiarize themselves with this work book.

The writer feels indebted to very many persons
who have assisted him and cheerfully utilizes this
opportunity to make due acknowledgments, Dr. Wil-
liam Rosenau, chairman of the Committee on Ele-
mentary Education and Dr. Joseph Rauch, both
members of the Commission on Jewish Education,
have read the manuscript carefully and have contributed many essential suggestions. Dr. Jacob R. Mar-
cus of the Faculty of the Hebrew Union College and
Dr. Isadore Keyfitz of the University of Missouri
have given the writer valuable critical help. The
writer is particularly grateful to his friend, Dr. Leo
L. Honor, Director of the College of Jewish Studies
of Chicago, who has read the manuscript very analyt-
ically and has contributed much, both to the verifi-
cation of fact and to the point of view. Mr. Solomon
Bluhm has kindly read the text and made suggestions for improvement in style, and Mr. Toby Kurz-
band was good enough to prepare the index.

Too often the technical workers, those who labor
thoughtfully over the form and appearance of the
volume, are entirely overlooked. At the present time,
when the construction of books has become an art
in its own right, we should be duly appreciative of
those who plan and execute the format of a volume.
The writer wishes to express his indebtedness to the
staff of the Union of American Hebrew Congrega-

tions, to Rabbi Louis I. Egelson for his painstaking collection of the numerous elements which go into a book, such as illustrations, maps, etc., to Mr. M. Myer Singer for his sensitive choice of typography, paper and binding, and for the general supervision of the book through the press; to Mr. Nelson Ronsheim for drawing the illustrations, maps, time lines and particularly for the attractive animated map inside of the book covers. The writer is particularly grateful to his friend, Dr. Emanuel Gamoran, educational director of the Commission on Jewish Education, for stimulating the work and for thoughtful reaction on numerous questions at issue. Lastly, the writer wishes to express his appreciation to the Union of American Hebrew Congregations for its liberality in the publication of this as of the prior volume, in sparing no expense to bring the book up to the finest standards of text-book making.

JACOB S. GOLUB

Cincinnati, Ohio.
June 10, 1930.

CONTENTS

Contents

SECTION IV

SECTION V

SECTION VI

Contents

vantage—The disadvantages, growth of social classes—Changes in law and justice.

PART II

Changes in religion, largely disadvantageous—The lowest layer imitates Canaanites—Upper layer develops Mosaic teachings—Priests of lower layer—Priest of Mosaic followers—Other religious ministers, early prophets are magicians—Prophets reprove kings—Another type of holy men, Nazarites—Where our ancestors worshipped—Feasts and Fasts—The religion of the average Israelite, a summary—Cultural progress, an advantage—War, gain and loss.

LIST OF MAPS

LIST OF ILLUSTRATIONS

Illustrations

Section I

Who Were Our Earliest
Ancestors?

A TIME LINE
ISRAEL AND SURROUNDING NATIONS

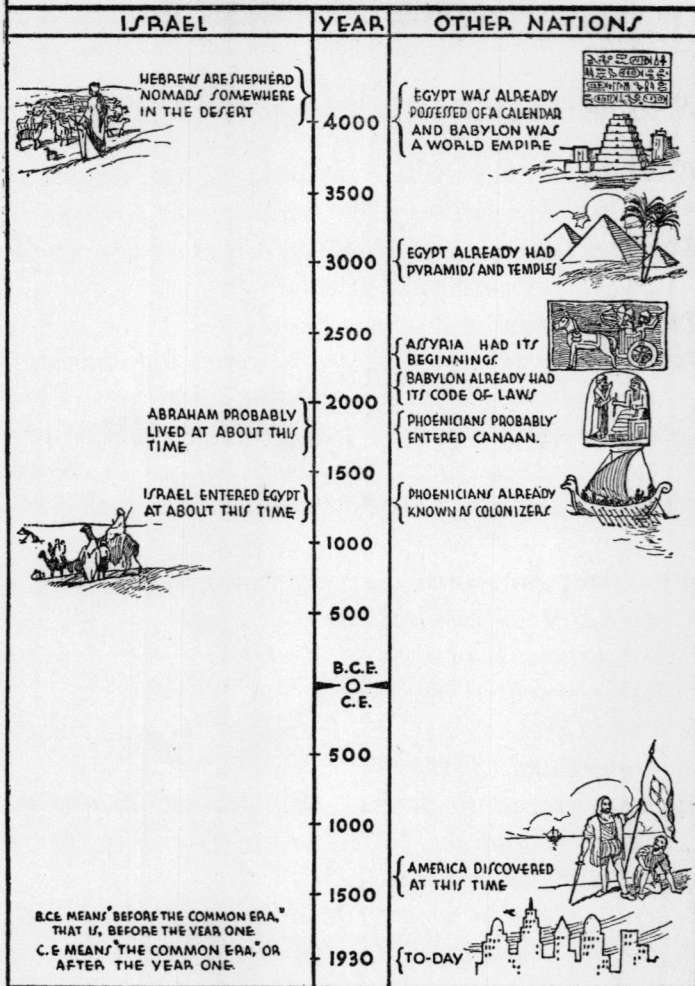

ISRAEL	YEAR	OTHER NATIONS
HEBREWS ARE SHEPHERD NOMADS SOMEWHERE IN THE DESERT	4000	EGYPT WAS ALREADY POSSESSED OF A CALENDAR AND BABYLON WAS A WORLD EMPIRE
	3500	
	3000	EGYPT ALREADY HAD PYRAMIDS AND TEMPLES
	2500	ASSYRIA HAD ITS BEGINNINGS
ABRAHAM PROBABLY LIVED AT ABOUT THIS TIME	2000	BABYLON ALREADY HAD ITS CODE OF LAWS / PHOENICIANS PROBABLY ENTERED CANAAN.
	1500	PHOENICIANS ALREADY KNOWN AS COLONIZERS
ISRAEL ENTERED EGYPT AT ABOUT THIS TIME	1000	
	500	
	B.C.E. O C.E.	
	500	
	1000	
	1500	AMERICA DISCOVERED AT THIS TIME
B.C.E. MEANS "BEFORE THE COMMON ERA," THAT IS, BEFORE THE YEAR ONE. C.E. MEANS "THE COMMON ERA," OR AFTER THE YEAR ONE.	1930	TO-DAY

WHO Were Our Earliest Ancestors?

*Where were they while Babylonia, Egypt, Assyria or
Phoenicia were already famous world powers?*
*Why did they not take their place sooner among the
important nations of history?*
This section will tell us the reason.
*It will show that in the earliest times our ancestors
were nomads or desert dwelling wanderers. Their
land being too poor to provide even sufficient pasture for their flocks, they were obliged to change
their camping grounds several times during the
year.*
*Wandering prevented our ancestors from reaching a
high state of civilization.*
*The constant hardships of desert life did develop
some excellent qualities in our forefathers.*
*It made them courageous; it trained them to endure
hunger and thirst.*
*Always exposed to danger, they learned to depend
upon one another, to feel brotherly and to regard
everyone as an equal.*
*Being so often in want of food and water, they felt
for the stranger and treated him hospitably.*
*But, altogether, nomads suffer many handicaps: in
lack of comforts; in the constant need of warfare;*

3

in being removed from contact with the rest of the world and thus developing a narrow range of ideas and beliefs about the world, about religion or even about their own past.

Therefore, as long as our ancestors were nomads, they could not hope to figure among the important peoples of the world.

As you read this section, remember that you are to answer the question which we have set at the head of this page.

DIGGING AMONG ANCIENT REMAINS

This picture shows how the ancient city of Gezer is being dug up. The city which was destroyed over two thousand years ago was long covered over with dirt and sand. Scientists, called archaeologists, try to guess where the ancient cities were located and then they hire workmen to dig the earth away, as you can see above.

4

Who Were Our Earliest Ancestors?

AROUND the eastern shores of the Mediterranean and beyond, where Europe meets Africa and Asia, there were once located the great empires of antiquity. These empires have long passed away. Yet men are still eagerly searching among their remains. Great scholars have been digging up the places where old cities are buried in the quest for articles or writings of ancient peoples. These records of a former day are so eagerly sought because in them may be read the story of how European civilization began.

What is *civilization*, you may ask. Although it sounds quite hard, it is a word that even young boys and girls can understand, if they try. By *civilization* we mean all the pleasant and useful ideas developed by man and all his discoveries and inventions. The discovery that fire would cook food, warm homes, forge weapons or aid in the making of finely wrought wares is an element of civilization. Learning to build homes, to care for our health, to make use of the

5

WHERE EUROPE
MEETS
AFRICA and ASIA

EMPIRES OF
ANTIQUITY

0   50   100   150   200
MILES

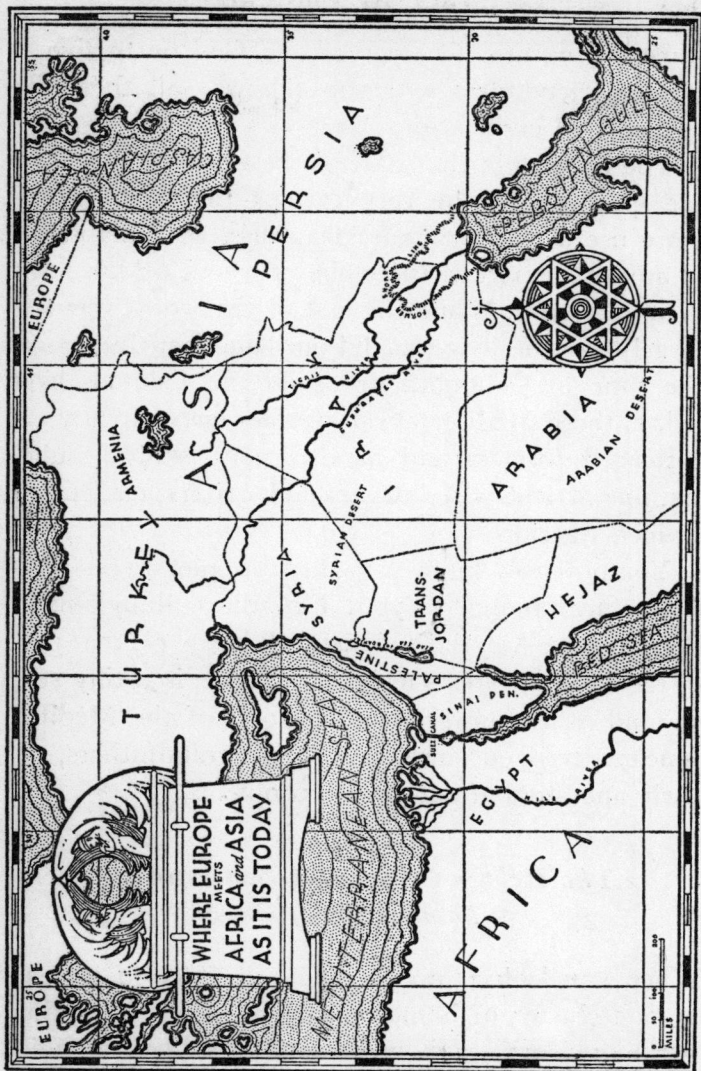

WHERE EUROPE
MEETS
AFRICA and ASIA
AS IT IS TODAY

forces of nature, to pray to one God or to live in greater friendliness with our fellows—all these are elements of civilization.

The peoples in that part of the world of which we are speaking, in the very earliest times thought of more useful and brilliant ideas than the inhabitants of any other part of the globe of whom we have any definite record. While the rest of the world was still largely savage, living as did our American Indians at the time of Columbus or as do the Eskimos even today, these Mediterranean peoples were already experienced farmers and handworkers, skillful builders, fine artists, wise lawyers and writers, and highly trained warriors.

You probably know who these peoples were. Their names are familiar to you: Egyptians, Babylonians, Phoenicians, Assyrians. Above all, however, that part of the world interests us because there, in a tiny strip of land on the lower eastern shores of the Mediterranean, lived our own great-great-grandfathers, the early ancestors of our Jewish people.

The Hebrews Were Latecomers in the Family of Nations

When you look at a city in the distance, it appears as one cluster of homes piled one above the other. A closer view may show, however, that houses which seemed to be very near each other are really separated by great distances. So the distant past may seem to many people a single period in which everything happened at about the same time. Yet these ancient days cover a space of many thousands of years. The history of Egypt extends back about twenty times as far as that of our United States. And even among the ancient peoples themselves there were old nations and young nations, some well established and some newcomers.

Look at the time line and note when our ancestors appear on the scene. You will readily see that Israel was among the newcomers in the ancient world. Egypt and Babylon had seen their greatest days before the Jewish nation was born. Egypt had already built her great temples and pyramids, and Babylon had worked out her law codes before our forefathers had made even the beginnings of a settled civilization. Our ancestors then began climbing the ladder of world civilization. One branch of civilization they developed far beyond any other people, and in the course of the centuries they also mastered the civilization of their neighbors.

Where Were the Hebrews During the Earlier Centuries?

What were our ancestors before they were known as Jews or Hebrews? Did they always live in Palestine? What prevented their becoming civilized sooner?

Where were they during the earlier centuries? Why did they not become known at that time like other peoples? What is a people before it becomes a full grown nation? How did our people grow up, and what finally helped it to set out on the road toward becoming one of the leading civilized nations of the world?

These questions we will undertake to answer in the first two sections of this book. The first section will attempt to tell what our ancestors were before they became a nation. The second section will tell how they took their first step toward nationhood.

Our Early Ancestors Nomads or Wanderers

In trying to describe our ancestors before they became a nation, we must bear in mind that we really have no certain knowledge of what happened at that early time. Our ancestors left no writings from that period. We have only stories, repeated by word of mouth from father to son over a period of hundreds of years, till they were finally written down in the Bible.

Judging from those stories, we may believe that our earliest ancestors were part of the wandering desert tribes who lived beyond the fertile sections. There were three fertile regions in the corner of the world of which we are speaking: the Mediterranean seacoast, Mesopotamia and Egypt. Around the fer-

A NOMADIC ENCAMPMENT TODAY

The Arab nomads still use the long square tent mainly. Most of
the tents are made from black goats' hair. Notice how the tents
are arranged in a circle for the protection of the animals during
the night.

tile sections stretched vast deserts, wastes of sand
or broken rock, with only here and there a bit of
pasture and a spring of water. Few of these desert
regions could support permanently settled peoples.
A tribe could live there only a few months. Then it
would have to gather its belongings and set out in
search of fresh camping grounds where there would
be grass for its cattle.

Hundreds of tribes inhabited and still do inhabit
the enormous Arabian Peninsula. Centuries pass

without any change in the life or habits of these
tribes. For this reason we speak of The Unchanging
East.

Sometimes, however, there is a famine or a war.
The tribe is deprived of even its scanty grass supply, and hunger drives the desert wanderers to
lands where nature appears more friendly. Thousands
upon thousands of desert men pour out upon the
more settled and fertile regions. If the invaded country is strong, the desert men are driven back. Otherwise, it is overpowered and its citizens become slaves
to the new conquerors.

Such great waves of migration, as the large invasions were called, occurred in Babylon, Egypt and
the surrounding lands. Similar migrations also
peopled early Greece, and later Rome and present
day Europe. Our own ancestors probably were contained in one of the great migrations which overran
Palestine or, as it was known then, the land of
Canaan.

How shall we know more about these desert tribesmen from whom we are sprung? We must attempt
a guess. The hints which the Bible gives lead us to
believe that desert dwellers in ancient times were
very much like similar peoples of today. We may,
therefore, secure a picture of the life of our earliest
ancestors by studying desert peoples of our own time
and seeing if what we learn resembles the kind of life
about which the Bible tells.

WHAT ARE THE DIFFERENCES BETWEEN DESERT DWELLERS AND PERSONS LIVING ON FERTILE LAND?

"A wandering Aramean was my father,"[1] says the Bible of the early Hebrews. Our earliest ancestors, as we have already suggested, were a desert-dwelling people. Now why are desert dwellers not as other peoples? Why are they not known among the important peoples of the earth?

Desert Dwellers Are Wanderers

One important difference is to be found in the fact that desert dwellers are nomads, or wanderers. They are persons who, as we have seen, have no fixed home or whose lands produce not even enough grass to support their flocks the entire year. Every few months such peoples must pull up stakes and wander on to new camping grounds. Good land or large oases are very scarce in the desert. If there are any fertile regions, the strongest tribes take possession of them. The weaker tribes must thus seek out other grazing lands which suffice only for a short part of the year.

We shall see why a people that is obliged to wander constantly in search of its food cannot become as highly civilized as one which has a fixed homeland.

[1] Deuteronomy, chap. VI, v. 5

Even among landless peoples there are many differing degrees. Hunting peoples are far less civilized than shepherd people. By comparison with some savage hunter tribes, such as the Bush Men of Australia, even our earliest forefathers were quite highly civilized. Peoples become more highly civilized when they have a definite way of earning their living. Farming peoples are safest because they raise their food from the soil. Shepherds can depend on their flocks. The savage hunters depend largely on chance or accident. If they are lucky in hunting game or in finding wild herbs they have food; otherwise they go hungry. Our forefathers were already possessed of domestic animals and may even have known a little of agriculture. However, by comparison with the great nations, shepherds do not rank very high in civilization.

Must Migrate in Small Groups

A nomadic people which wanders from place to place is, of necessity, much smaller than a settled nation. You can readily imagine how impossible it would be for a nation of forty or fifty million people to find new homes frequently. It would be difficult even for one million people to wander about the desert in a single group. The oases are seldom larger than small villages, while the flocks need wide meadows for grazing. It must be clear that a nomadic company or clan cannot be large.

TRAVEL IN PALESTINE

To this day the Arab of Palestine travels as desert men did thousands of years ago. The loaded camels carry the household goods as well as the women and children. Notice the little donkey which was the animal mainly used by men. Horses, in ancient times, were used mainly for purposes of war.

Let us join one of the companies of our ancestors and live with it during a period of wandering. The band is on the march, carrying with it all its wealth, which consists of a flock of animals driven in front and of household goods packed on the backs of the camels. Nothing else can the tribe call its own. On the backs of the camels are its houses, its furniture, its dishes and food—everything that its members might need or want.

How surprisingly small the tribe is and what little property it possesses. The United States consists of

120,000,000 persons. The Jews, who are considered a small people, at present consist of fifteen or sixteen millions. Our earliest ancestors, as we have suggested, numbered not one million, nor one half, nor even a quarter million. Each company may have numbered not more than one or two thousand, fewer persons than one finds in one crowded city block. The larger Jewish people grew out of these small bands, as all other nations grew from their small beginnings.

They Are Organized into Clans

We call these groups, these bands of our ancestors, *clans*. Clans are very large families made up of a number of smaller families who claim descent from a common ancestor. The head of the clan was called the Father or Patriarch, the father-chief. The clan usually consisted of the following persons: the father, his wives and their young children; the grown sons with

A NOMADIC FAMILY

As it lives in its tent-home today, just as our ancestors did thousands of years ago.

their wives and children; the sons' married sons, if there were any, and their wives and children; uncles, aunts, and cousins with their families. In addition, there were the slaves who were, however, considered as much a part of the family as were the children. Occasionally, too, there were exiles or fugitives who may have left their own families because their chief was too severe or because they desired to unite with a stronger clan. Just so today, many persons from foreign countries come to the United States to join it rather than remain citizens of their native lands.

The larger the family, the more capable was it of defending itself against other families. So long, therefore, as there was sufficient food, the father was very happy to admit new persons into the clan. He would thus spare the lives of prisoners of war and make them slaves. Strangers might be adopted as free members of the household. Additional wives for the chief or his sons might further add to the numbers in the clan. When food was scarce, no stranger was admitted, and all war prisoners were killed. Sometimes those members of the clan who could not serve in fighting or in getting food were killed, to preserve food for the others. When the family became too large and the grazing grounds too small for them, the clan divided into two clans, each seeking its own pastures. Such an incident is the Bible story of the separation of Abraham and Lot. [1]

[1] Genesis, chap. XIII

The Clan a Family Nation

The clan was a family government. The father was the supreme ruler, enjoying the rights which kings at that time had over their subjects. He could punish any member of his family by expelling him from the clan, as we find in the story of Abraham and Ishmael. The Patriarch had the power to sentence an offender to death. He acted as judge in quarrels within the family, as priest at religious gatherings, and as chief in war and peace. His authority included the right to choose wives for his sons and husbands for his daughters. His power was limited only by the customs which had grown up for hundreds of years and which the whole clan had to obey. Such laws were mostly of a religious nature, the violation of which was considered an insult to the gods. One of these strict laws referred to the welcome given a stranger by members of the clan. A wanderer, received in the tent of a tribesman and sharing his food and water, thereby became a friend and ally of the whole family, and no harm might be done him thereafter. Even the head of the family could not overstep this rule.

OLDEST SON RANKS SECOND

The person next in importance, as you may readily guess, was the one who would become leader of the family after the father's death, namely, the eldest son of the chief wife. The eldest son occupied a position like that of a crown prince. Next to the father, he was responsible for the household and had to protect its interests. His advice was listened to with great respect among his brothers. He looked after the household gods and he was usually considered sacred and belonging to the gods.

The right of being considered the first born, called the birthright, belonged to the oldest son; but he could sell it or he might give it away, the buyer thus undertaking all the duties and receiving all the privileges. You probably remember the story of how Esau sold his birthright to Jacob for a pot of lentils.[1]

The other members of the family were ranked according to their sex and their state of freedom. Men were considered of much greater importance than women, who were treated almost like slaves. Since they could not go to war, women were obliged to do all the hard work at home and in the pasture.

SLAVES WERE PART OF FAMILY

Slaves were not very common among nomadic peoples, unless the clan was large and wealthy. As among settled peoples, slaves generally prisoners of war whose lives had been spared, were counted with the domestic animals. They were put to hard labor,

[1] Genesis, chap. XXVI, 29 ff.

JACOB BLESSES ISAAC

After Doré

and like animals, could be sold or exchanged. In the small clan, however, the slave was often treated as a member of the family. Slaves with exceptional ability could even rise to important posts, such as stewards of the clan. Eliezer of Damascus was in charge of Abraham's household and, had Isaac not been born, would have become the patriarch in place of Abraham.

The free men of the family were the important citizens. They met in council in war and peace. They discussed all important undertakings, and though the father was not obliged to act upon their advice, he usually consulted them. The men of the clan enjoyed much more freedom and independence than one is accustomed to think of in a country ruled by an absolute monarch.

DISADVANTAGES OF CLAN LIFE—IN EARNING A LIVING

Living within a small family clan has many disadvantages not found among a larger people. An outstanding disadvantage of clan life arises from the very limited opportunities of earning a livelihood. Within the small clan persons did not have as wide a choice of occupations as we have today. Some occupations were restricted to men and some to women. Every man was expected to be familiar with all of the men's occupations, and every woman had to know

NOMADIC OCCUPATIONS

Modern Bedouins and a butter churn made out of goat skin. Life in the East has changed little during the past three thousand years.

all female tasks. Naturally, persons developed greater skill at some one occupation than at others, but in general the whole clan worked together; everything that was made belonged to the clan as a whole, each member receiving from the clan what he needed in food or clothing.

Occupations Few

The trades in which the members of the clan engaged were not numerous or complicated, being devoted mainly to obtaining food and clothing. The chief occupation was the tending of flocks, of camels, donkeys, sheep and goats. The animals furnished dairy foods and wool and hair for spinning and weaving clothes, mats and tents. When the tribe had more of these products than it needed, it exchanged them with passing merchants for clay pots or trinkets and with the farmer for grain and vegetables.

The tending of the sheep was usually left to the

men, though women, too, were known to be shep-
herdesses. You may recall the story of how Jacob
met Rachel coming to the well with her father's
flocks, or of the meeting of Moses with the daughter
of Jethro. However, aside from tending the flocks,
which seemed to be a common occupation, the other
labors were rather clearly divided. The chief work of
the women concerned itself with the home. They did
the cooking, the baking and the weaving. They
ground the flour and carried the water from the well.

A HAND MILL FOR GRINDING CORN

In certain parts of Palestine, women still grind corn as they used
to in olden times. The grain is poured in through a hole in the
center of the upper stone and is ground between the two stones.

The men on their part sheared the wool or slaughtered the animals, whenever they were to have meat. They tanned the hides and made sandals, straps and rough saddles, as well as bottles for water and for wine. They made bows, arrows and slings. Considerable skill was shown in working in wood, making arrows, spears, handles and saddle frames.

Labor Is Hard

Though the tasks of the wandering nomad were few and simple, they were not at all light or easy. On the contrary, the work of the shepherd was very hard. In the stories of Jacob and Laban we have a description of the work of the shepherd. Jacob complains that all day long he is exposed to the blazing sun, while at night he may not seek shelter against the frost, for he must always be on guard against wild animals, in which the land abounds, or against thieves, who were equally common and more dangerous. Jacob declares that he can no longer sleep, so worn has he become from his work. Yet his was the work of an ordinary shepherd.

It is likely that not all the tribes were merely tenders of cattle. Several of the tribes were probably semi-nomadic, that is, engaged for part of the year in tilling the soil. The Bible speaks of some of the Hebrews as living in the region south of Hebron, which is called the *Negeb* or dry land, but which is not entirely a desert. In years of abundant rainfall some of the *Negeb* could be cultivated. Thus we are told in the Bible that Isaac raised crops. Such agriculture, however, was very simple and did not produce enough for the entire year. Part of the year the clan still had to migrate in search of grazing land.

Meager Returns for Hard Labor—In Shelter

In return for this hard labor the nomad enjoyed little of life's comforts. He often had the hard ground for his bed and a few figs for his day's food.

Our forefathers' homes were in tents, the only kind of dwelling which can be moved easily from place to place. The wealthier the tribe, the more tents it owned. The tent was generally partitioned by a curtain, one side reserved for the men and the other for the women and children. The more important members of the clan probably had separate tents for the men and the women.

IN FURNISHINGS

The furnishings within the tent were scanty and crude. On the floor there were several mats of straw or of goat's hair, which served as beds at night and as seats in the day time. In place of a table was a round piece of leather, with several holes near the border through which a cord might be drawn. After

A MODERN BAKING OVEN

The oven is a clay cylinder, open at the top. The fire is made below and the bread-cakes are pasted about the sides above. The front part is cut away merely to show what the inside looks like.

the meal the leather was folded as a bag, in which food was carried on the journeys.

The clan possessed some baking o v e n s, which consisted of clay basins with a hole in the center. When baking, the women pasted the dough on the sides of the basin, which was turned over and covered with live coals. Every clan, too, possessed mill-stones for grinding corn into flour. In addition, there were a few leather bottles, in which to carry milk and butter, and some earthen pots or jars. These constituted the nomads' entire house furnishings. Think of all the articles found in even a single room of any house today, no matter how poor, and you will realize how hard life must have been for the wandering man of three or four thousand years ago.

The tent, besides housing a human family, often served as a shelter for the animal young. Nomads had no objection to their favorite animals sleeping in the same tent with them. Even to this day the Arab will frequently bring his camel into his tent. The nomads were too poor, however, to provide shelter for all their flocks. When they pitched their tents, therefore, they usually arranged them in a circle, the animals being kept within the enclosure as a protection against beasts of prey and robbers.

IN CLOTHES

The nomads wore very few garments. These were made of coarse wool. Next to the skin the nomad wore an undershirt, which was open at the front and tied with a girdle about the waist. The openings of the shirt were used as two big pockets which were made to hold anything from food to little children or lambs. Above the undershirt was a tunic, reaching a little above the knees. Above the tunic was the cloak or coat which was nothing more than a large blanket-shaped cloth, such as you may have observed

THE INSIDE OF THE TENT

This is the women's and children's quarters. Today, as in the past, the family squats on the floor. Notice that the tent is not a very comfortable shelter either against heat or desert storms.

the Indians wear-
ing. The outer gar-
ment usually had
bright stripes at
the ends. This
cloak was put to
many uses. It
served as a coat by
day and a blanket
by night; or it
might be a bag in
which to carry
loads or a fodder
bag out of which
to feed the ani-
mals. On their feet

MODERN BEDOUIN CHIEFS
They are always armed and ready for
war or raid. Notice their garments
which resemble those worn by our
ancestors except for the cartridge
belts, of course.

they wore sandals tied with leather cords. Their
heads were shaded from the sun by means of a
piece of heavy cloth tied about the forehead with
a string.

IN FOOD

Their food, as we have already mentioned, was
very plain. Bread, made of barley flour, and dairy
products were their chief foods. Only on an important occasion did they kill an animal for meat. In
addition, they used the natural products of the
deserts, such as figs and dates.

Obviously the life of the nomads was severe, being subject to frequent hunger and thirst. Even his meager comforts were often interfered with. His water might contain poisonous snakes or leeches, the grazing grounds might be haunted by wild beasts or contested for by other clans.

The only sense of comfort which the nomad enjoyed was the feeling that the entire clan shared his dangers. When there was enough food, everybody was fed; when food was scarce, everyone suffered hunger alike. Common misfortunes are usually borne more easily.

Frequent Warfare

Another disadvantage of life in a small clan is the constant fear of other clans. Even the few comforts which are obtained at such great hardship must be constantly guarded against raids. Every other clan, unless bound by an alliance, is a possible enemy, to be watched and attacked whenever the opportunity presents itself.

The nomads' hostility to other peoples is well expressed in the Biblical expression "His hand (is) against every man, and every man's hand (is) against him." [1]

In the course of their warlike operations it is a common practice for nomads to waylay caravans

[1] Genesis, chap. XVI, v. 12

on the highroad and to exact a ransom for the right
of way. To this day nomads make it as unsafe to
cross the desert without sufficient guard as it was
several thousand years ago. The nomad, like the
brave knight of the Middle Ages, believed that whatever he could capture by his sword was his by
right of conquest.

BRINGS OUT UNPLEASANT QUALITIES

Warfare brings out unpleasant qualities in people.
It makes them cruel, sly, cunning, always plotting to
fool their enemies. We may better understand the
feeling of nomadic people if we bear in mind that
even today among so-called civilized nations we do
not think it wrong to fool our enemies. The cleverer
we are in deceiving the enemy in wartime, the
greater praise do we receive. The nomad, being so
often at war, tends to grow into wartime habits even
in his everyday life. That is why people of lower
civilization are so often cruel.

Might decided what was right in the desert. The
tribe that was not strong was in danger of extermi-
nation or of being sold into slavery. Because of the
constant danger of attack, every man was a soldier,
while the chief was the bravest and strongest man of
the tribe. Some ancient peoples even practiced a custom of exposing the old and the crippled to death,
since these were of no use in war. That, however,

seems not to have been the practice of our Hebrew ancestors.

AT WAR EARLY

We do not know the exact age at which a young man became a warrior. In later times the age was twenty. He was furnished with the weapons of his tribe and he joined the men in their campaigns. The nomad's equipment consisted in olden times, as to-day, of a fast mount, either a horse or a camel, and a long spear. Nomads never move in large armies, there being probably no more than several hundred in any one company. (We have in the Bible the example of Abraham who defeated four kings with a troop of 318 men.) Their method of fighting consists of making a raid and then fleeing with their booty as fast as possible. Their equipment, therefore, had to be very light. In addition to the spear, they carried bows and arrows and probably slings, which, in later times, David used with effect.

The results of nomadic wars were often more deadly than the battles themselves. Falling into the enemy's hands was a disgrace, and prisoners of war were treated accordingly. It was the practice of the nomads to mutilate their prisoners by blinding the victims, cutting off the fighting fingers or clipping the ear tips. Such a disfigured person always carried about with him the sign of having permitted himself to be taken prisoner. More frequently all male prisoners were put to death. The victorious clan would often kill all the enemy fighting men, taking the women and children as captives.

Thus the clan might hardly enjoy peacefully even the little that fell to its share.

Responsibility for Avenging Fellow Members

Another result of the nomads' constant warfare is the responsibility which the members of the clan feel for each other's safety. The code of every nomadic group requires all members to defend one another against strangers. It does not matter who is in the wrong, the clan keeps together as does a boys' gang. The situation becomes very serious if one of the clansmen is slain. His entire tribe must seek revenge against the whole clan of the murderer. A blood feud thus starts, in the course of which any member of one clan is obliged to kill any member of the other. A whole clan might thus be exterminated as shown in the Bible story of the war with Amalek. Often, however, peace is made by offering satisfaction to the injured family in the form of gifts.

RIGHTS ENFORCED WITHIN THE CLAN

However, though the nomads were ever ready to avenge their comrades, let us not assume that there was no law or justice within the clan. In the case where one member injured another a very severe law was applied, known by its Latin name as *lex talionis,* or the law of doing the same (retaliation). "But if any harm follow, then thou shalt give life for life, eye for eye, tooth for tooth." [1] Thus, one who knocked out a tooth of his opponent would himself meet with a like fate; if he burned another person, he, too, was burned.

In later Jewish life, we shall find, these harsh measures were greatly modified by law. In place of taking out the offender's eye or tooth, a money fine was substituted.

It may be well for us to know that even the *lex talionis* was a step in advance, for at an earlier time, the penalty for injuring one's fellow tribesman was death. The change of the law, to inflict upon the offender only as severe an injury as that which he had caused, was already an important move toward greater justice.

FINER SIDE OF NOMADIC CHARACTER—HOSPITALITY

Let us not imagine, however, that the nomad was a fierce savage who killed every stranger at sight. When not at war, in the shelter of his own tent, the nomad was generally kindly. Indeed, the customs of his tribe required him to be friendly even to strangers.

[1] Exodus, chap. XXI, v. 23, 24

Thus, while on the warpath the nomad was every man's enemy, in his tent he might be any man's friend. He befriended a person not in return for a favor he had received, but because he had himself done a kindness to the stranger. Such was the law of the desert.

If any man came into a tent and asked for a drink of water, which was the usual form of asking for something to eat or drink, he became at once the friend of the man whose tent he entered. He was given free food and shelter for three days.

ABRAHAM RECEIVING STRANGERS

Illustrating the famous story of desert hospitality—as the artist imagined it.

If he chose to remain longer, he was expected to assist the other men at work.

To this day, when a man is in danger, if pursued, for example, by a band of robbers, he will run to a tent of some powerful chief. Once in the tent of the chief, he becomes the ally of the whole tribe, whose duty it now is to defend him.

A traveler in modern Arabia tells of a very interesting experience in the East. Being attacked in the desert by a group of Arabs, he fled for safety to an encampment which he saw in the distance. After receiving the customary hospitality, he discovered to his amazement that he had sought shelter in the camp of his pursuers; but having shared their food and water, he became their ally and they were now bound to defend him.

Examples in Bible

The Bible contains several beautiful stories of our ancestors' hospitality. Abraham, the Patriarch, sitting at the entrance of his tent in the heat of the day, sees three passing strangers. He prostrates himself before them on the ground, offering them the comfort of his tent. He himself hastens to prepare the feast for them, slaughtering a choice heifer in their honor, and gladly serves them while they eat.[1]

To this day our religion commands us to be hos-

[1] Genesis, chap. XVIII

pitable like our forefather Abraham. Lot bravely
risks the attacks of all his townsmen rather than
permit them to do harm to his guests.[1] The punishment that Sodom and Gomorrah received, the
legend tells us, was partly due to their abuse of
the law of hospitality.

DIFFICULT LIFE OF NOMADS PREVENTS GROWTH OF IDEAS

The nomad's difficult struggle to earn his livelihood
and his constant occupation with fighting prevent him
from learning new ways of life or from getting new
ideas and thoughts. He is too tired after his day's
labors or feels himself too much in danger to risk
trying new ways or beliefs.

Thus in many ways the nomads were simple, be-
having much like children. When they were happy
or when they were distressed, they showed their joy
or sorrow publicly. Men on meeting kissed each
other, or as another form of greeting shook each
other's beards. At the death of a member of the
family, the relatives would try to outdo each other
in weeping and lamentation.

It is told by modern travelers through Arabia
that even to this day, after a guest has had a meal
in his host's tent, he will begin to groan and make
sounds as though he were choking, to show that he

[1] Genesis, chap. XIX

has eaten his fill and cannot possibly have any more. It would be considered a sign of disrespect on the part of the guest if he failed to make the display of having dined sufficiently.

Nomadic Religion—Ideas of God

The simplicity of nomads' ideas is best illustrated in their religion. Since religion is so important to us as Jews, our people having been among the world's greatest religious teachers, let us proceed to gather what notions we can about the religion of early nomadic peoples.

We today worship one God who, we believe, rules the entire world. Although there are many different nations, speaking various languages, we yet believe that God is our common father and that all men are brothers.

The nations of antiquity thought differently of their god. Our own ancestors, who were to teach the belief of one God to the rest of the world required many centuries to learn this belief. Let us examine some of the earlier ideas which our forefathers had to outgrow.

We have already seen that the early Hebrews consisted of many clans, some entirely and some only partly nomadic. The surroundings in which a particular clan lived and its closeness to a more highly civilized settlement affected its religion.

NOMADS WORSHIP SPIRITS

The desert-dwelling clans might be expected to have
a very *naive* or childlike religion. They believed that
the world was filled with spirits, good and evil, the
good spirits being interested in helping men, and the
bad spirits or demons seeking an opportunity to do
them harm. These spirits were said to live in oases,
springs, unusually shaped rocks or large trees. You
have probably read stories of fairies, brownies, elves
or Jack-o-lanterns. Desert peoples believed that these
various kinds of spirits really existed. Whoever kept
on friendly terms with them they would not hurt—
they might even help him; otherwise the spirits
might do much mischief.

The way to keep on good terms with the spirits
was to bring them food or drink. Such gifts were
hung on the branches of the tree or left near the
rock or the spring supposedly inhabited by the
spirits. The presentation of such offerings you may
be interested to know, is still practiced among the
simple Arabs of Palestine.

The dead, too, according to these beliefs, became
spirits and, therefore, objects of fear and worship.
Many persons still fear ghosts. This is naught but
the remains of the ancient worship of the dead. The
departed had prayers addressed to them and feasts
arranged in their honor. Stones were placed over the

graves and, as we shall see presently, these were used in the practice of religion.

LOCAL GODS WORSHIPPED

The spirits of the springs, trees or groves were believed to possess only their special dwellings. Wandering nomads, whose life depended on the spring or oasis, could well think of its possessor as the highest power. The semi-nomads who lived near settled peoples were influenced by their neighbors in their ideas of God. The settled peoples, occupying a large territory, naturally pictured their gods as more than mere owners of a spring or tree. Their gods were thought of as the owners of their entire land, directing the weather, the rain, the sunshine or the moonlight. However, even settled peoples limited the gods to their own districts.

Each separate nation had its own god or gods, who exercised power only within the boundaries of their own lands. A man entering a new country left the worship of his native god behind and adopted the service of the god of the country in which he found himself.

It was not at all unusual for each of several sections within one country to have its own gods. In time the worship of one particular god became dominant and he came to be regarded as the king or the father of the gods. We can see how in time people might arrive at the next step of thinking that at least in their own land only the chief god was really a god and the lesser gods were only spirits.

The half-nomadic Hebrew tribes living near Canaan very likely accepted a religion like that of their neighbors. Many of the clans probably worshipped one of the numerous local gods. Some of them, however, very early became distinguished as the worshippers of the main god. They did not deny the existence of other gods, nor did they believe that their god ruled outside of Canaan; but they believed their God stronger and more helpful than other gods and, therefore, they were his worshippers.

We might thus say that among our earliest ancestors there were some clans that worshipped spirits or demons; others, worshipping their particular gods, considered them the equals of the gods of other peoples; and a small group may have believed that, while there were other gods in the world, its god was the greatest or mightiest of all. Those who worshipped the higher gods did not abandon the belief in good and bad spirits or the worship of the dead. All spirits had to be given their due; but, above all, they were concerned with the worship of their one God.

The Nature of God

We think of our God as good, kind and just. We believe that our God commands us to do the right, and that the only way to please God is through acts of righteousness. The gods of our early ancestors, like their spirits, were imagined differently. The gods were thought of as great chiefs, more powerful than their rulers and, like them, loving to fight and to feast. Just as the tribesman brought a gift to his chief when making a request of him, so he felt that in approaching his gods his desires would be granted if his prayers were accompanied with gifts. It was less important to act kindly or to be upright than to bring a sufficient offering.

Besides, just as every chief or ancient king desired to be ruler over as large a country and population as possible, so, it was thought, their god-chief was anxious to extend his dominions. Accordingly, wars were frequently waged to prove the superiority of one god over another and to add to his territory.

The Appearance of God

Since the ancients thought of God as a great chief, we might imagine that they pictured him as a mighty man, tall, muscular and fierce, inspiring fear among his attendants and retainers. They might have thought of him as inhabiting a beautiful tent or house and as living in great luxury.

That, however, was not the way in which early peoples pictured their god. They thought of him in a way that seems strange to us. The ancient peoples

GODS PICTURED WITH ANIMAL HEADS

These four are Egyptian gods. From left to right they are: Sekhmat, the war god; Anubis, ruler of the lower world; Chnoum, father of the gods; and Ammon, the sun god.

generally pictured their gods as animals or as human figures with the heads of animals. Such was the custom of nomadic tribes all over the world, not only among the nomads in the Syrian desert, but also among the civilized men of Africa and Australia and among the American Indians. Even such highly civilized countries as Egypt and Babylon represented their gods in a similar manner.

Where God Lived: How to Find God

Our God is everywhere. "The heavens are My throne and the earth is My footstool," says the prophet about God. We need not go elsewhere to seek God. Whenever and wherever we think of Him, He is with us. For the men of long ago, however, it was impossible to imagine how God could do without a home. Nor could they understand how God can be everywhere at the same time. Their god, being a very important being, might have many homes which he visited at various occasions. It was helpful to know all his haunts, and particularly to be certain when he might be found at each of his residences. The tops of high mountains were considered to be favored dwellings for the gods. They were also believed to reside in places formerly connected with spirits of lesser importance, in sacred groves of oaks, in a single oak, in palm trees, in wells of water or in large solitary stones.

At these places the nomads gathered to offer sacrifices or gifts to the gods, to sing, dance, have races, games and feasts, as the Arabs of the desert still do to this day.

All places of worship, as already mentioned, were in the open air. In connection with the worship of spirits there were probably few ceremonies. The worshippers would come to the place where the spirit was believed to be and, placing gifts near the spring or on the branches of the tree, would make their request.

HIGH PLACES

The worship of the gods was more organized. Like the spirits, the gods were as yet worshipped in the open air, at the holy place or *high place,* as it was called. The high place usually contained an altar on which gifts to the gods were placed. The altar was either a large rock or a bed of earth. In the rock altars which were found among the ancient remains there are cup shaped holes, the exact purpose of which we do not know. They may have been used either to contain drink offerings of wine, oil or blood, or to hold cone shaped vessels in which food was brought to the gods. The rocks also show channels cut into them to carry off the blood of animals which were killed as a sacrifice. Besides the altar, the high

ALTAR WITH CUP HOLES
In which pointed jars could be placed containing food or drink
for the gods.

place contained a
pillar of rough
stone, from six to
ten feet in height,
over which oil was
poured. Important
high places might
have several pil-
lars. At some, cir-
cles of stone also
were found, the
purpose of which
we do not know.

AN ANCIENT HIGH PLACE

Notice the two stone pillars or *Maze-bahs*. These two stones were found at Taanach, near the Valley of Jezreel. They were over a cave and near them was found a statue of the goddess Astarte.

Sacred Trees

Besides the pillar,
called the *Mazebah,* there generally stood the sacred
tree or symbol of a tree, such as a stump or a post.
The tree was the symbol of the mother Astarte, and
was called the *Asherah.*

The Bible frequently mentions the pillar or *Maze-bah* in connection with acts of worship by Jacob, but
it is not clear whether the *Asherah*, or tree, was also
used. In later times we shall see that the Hebrews
copied the complete form of Canaanite worship, but
we do not as yet know clearly how far the Hebrew
high place at this time resembled that of their neighbors.

Occasionally a tribesman desires to pray urgently while his god might be at some distant home, too far away to reach readily. A simple way of having the god always near at hand was to make a picture or a likeness of the god, which we now call an idol. Pictures were believed to possess magic powers of the person represented. Thus, if you hoped to hurt your enemy, you might make a wax figure of him and stab the figure or burn it. Similarly the likeness of the god was believed to be possessed of the powers of the god.

When people prayed to the image, or idol, they did not really worship wood or stone. They knew that the idols were only likenesses of the gods, but they thought that the likeness had a special power or magic given it by the god of whom it was an image. The likeness, to be powerful or magical, had to be done according to fixed rules. In Egypt, for example, the gods, or the Pharaohs who were considered very close to the gods, could be carved only in certain poses.

Priests, Magic and Magicians

In every household or clan the chief was also the high priest. God was the earliest father of the clan; therefore, the present chief-father was the natural person who might be in closest friendship with him. There were, however, other spirits that might do harm, if not properly worshipped. If a person became ill, it was believed to be the work of an evil spirit. If one's arrows failed of their mark, an evil spirit had loosened the bow strings. If the well dried up, an evil spirit had taken the water away. A special group of men, called magicians or soothsayers, were believed to have power over the spirits. By muttering certain sounds or performing various acts and dances, they were considered able either to persuade the spirit to leave peaceably or to drive him out by force.

Sometimes a magician might be called to ask the evil spirit to do harm to the enemy. We have in the Bible the story of Balaam, who is asked by Balak, the king of Moab, to curse the Israelites. Balaam, however, finds that the God of Israel is too strong for his spirits.

SUPERSTITIONS

Uncivilized peoples believed very strongly in good and bad luck, as do many civilized persons even today. The beliefs that a found penny is lucky, that 13 is an unlucky number, that it is bad to cross the path of a black cat or that one should not move into a new house on Monday, are examples of modern superstition. You may still hear some good people say *"Kein ayin ho-rah,"* which means, may no evil eye hurt the person of whom they may be telling

AMULETS

Usually beetles or scarabs, or blue beads to ward off evil spirits.

something flattering. In ancient times there were thousands of such superstitions which people feared. Many happenings which to us would seem most ordinary were accepted as divine signs or omens. Stumbling against a rock was considered a sign of approaching evil. Dreams were warnings of God foretelling the future. The crowing of the cock or the bleating of an animal was considered significant. If a man on a journey saw two sticks crossed, it might be a warning to return home immediately.

There were ways of warding off bad luck. One might wear a charm or amulet which usually represented an image or symbol of a god. Most of the jewelry worn by nomads and by later Israelites were amulets containing pictures of Egyptian gods or, often, of various insects. Blue beads were particularly popular as charms. Such a charm or amulet was considered powerful enough to keep evil spirits away from its wearer forever. Often big charms were necessary for the whole tribe. In case of a public calamity, such as the failure of rain, all the magicians would gather, dance and shriek, cut their flesh, and pronounce their most powerful magic. Then, if rain came, they asserted their charms had worked. If they were unsuccessful, they might insist someone had interrupted the workings of the magic by wrong or evil thoughts.

When a person became ill, an enemy might be accused of having bewitched him. A special magician, the witch doctor, would then be sent for to find the one who had bewitched the sick man. Whoever was thus accused had little chance of convincing anyone of his innocence. His fate usually was death.

Such were some of the beliefs of our ancestors in the very beginning of our history. They appear to be so childlike that we wonder how grown persons could ever have held them. We must bear in mind, however, that the whole world began in the same way, and that there are still millions of people in all the five continents who think of their god or gods as did our ancestors of old. We, on our part, may look back with pride upon forefathers who, beginning so humbly, rose so far above the other peoples of their day in their idea of God that they could become the teachers of religion to the world.

SUMMARY

We are now ready to answer the questions which we set forth at the beginning of this section. What sort of people were our ancestors before they became a nation, and why were they not sooner known in history? They were small nomadic clans, seeking to gain a livelihood by tending flocks in the desert. Their wandering, their hard toil, the constant fear of raid and preparation for attack kept them a small unnoticed people of simple beliefs and customs. There was as yet no reason why any of the great nations should take notice of them. Nor did they themselves possess either the skill of writing so that they could tell of their own adventures, or any distinctive manufactures, pottery, trinkets or weapons, from the remains of which we might learn some facts about them.

What Records Did Our Ancestors Leave?

Our earliest ancestors did leave us some information about themselves. Even the clan wished to know what happened in the days before. Nations, like persons, are interested in their past. Only very young infants, who cannot remember, and the lowest races of men have no stories of their earlier days. Our ancestors, even at the dawn of our history, entertained some ideas of their origins. Their accounts may not have been very accurate, because the science of exact history did not yet exist. Nor could they preserve a record in writing because, as we have told, they were as yet unable to write. Their stories were re-

THE STORY CIRCLE

To this day the story is a favorite entertainment after the evening meal. During such story hours the tales of Israel's past were handed down from father to son till they were finally written down in the Bible.

membered orally and retold at camp fires by the patriarch or by professional story-tellers, who were interested mainly in entertaining their listeners with tales of adventure.

The stories thus repeated from memory would undergo many changes, since each story-teller felt free to enlarge or to modify the story to make it more interesting. In this way unimportant periods were forgotten, because there was little to tell of them, and great names were made to follow one an-

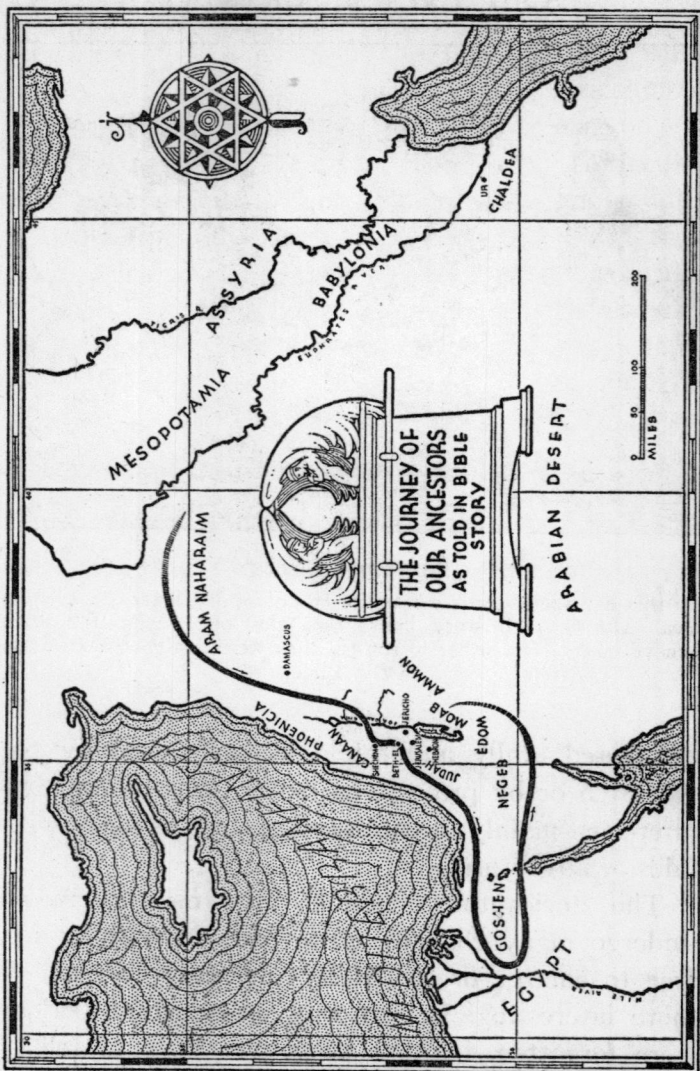

THE JOURNEY OF
OUR ANCESTORS
AS TOLD IN BIBLE
STORY

MESOPOTAMIA

ASSYRIA

BABYLONIA

CHALDEA

UR

EUPHRATES RIVER

ARABIAN DESERT

ARAM NAHARAIM

DAMASCUS

PHOENICIA

CANAAN

JUDAH

MOAB

AMMON

EDOM

NEGEB

GOSHEN

EGYPT

NILE RIVER

MILES
0   50   100   200

other as though all the famous chiefs of old were sons or brothers.

You are undoubtedly familiar with the early patriarchs from your study of Bible stories. The Bible stories were written down a thousand or more years after they had supposedly happened, so that much legend has gathered about the original history. Attempting, therefore, to reconstruct a picture of what really happened, the following seems a likely account.

Abraham

The first group of Hebrews under a leader, Abraham, left its home in Chaldea or more probably Aram Naharaim, the northern portion of Mesopotamia, and traveled toward Canaan at about 1800 B.C.E. The people entered Canaan at Shechem, one of the gateways to the new land. The inhabitants of the region, though powerless to halt the march of the Hebrews, were strong enough to prevent them from settling in their midst, and forced the migration southward toward the Negeb.

The Negeb, the district south of Judah, lies between Canaan and the desert. It is half desert, containing few springs and scanty grass; and, though it may possibly have been more fertile in ancient times, it was even then known as the dry land. There Abraham's tribe seems to have found camping grounds;

but the insufficiency of pasture land caused serious disputes between the clans, finally forcing some of them to break away in search of new homes. The Bible represents these quarrels as disagreements between Abraham and Lot, which in the end led to the formation of the kingdoms of Ammon and Moab by the descendants of Lot. The Abraham tribe continued to lead a nomadic life in the Negeb. In time of famine it migrated to Egypt, but was unable to remain there.

There is mention of war between the Hebrews and their neighbors over springs of water; but peace was established, and the right of the Hebrews to their camping grounds seemed confirmed by the sale of a burial cave to Abraham in Hebron.

HEBREWS ON MARCH

Of Abram's son, Isaac, very little is reported except that he had two sons who apparently did not live peaceably together. The flight of Jacob from Esau may mean that wars broke out among the Hebrew tribes, as a result of which some of them returned to their original Aramean home while others established themselves as the nation of Edom, south of the Dead Sea.

Jacob

The history of the Hebrews seems to begin anew with Jacob's travels to Canaan. Historians believe that the return of Jacob meant the migration of a new group of Hebrew tribes, twelve in number, who called themselves Bnai Jacob or Bnai Israel. Each of the tribes is represented as one man, a son of Jacob, in accordance with the general ancient practice of describing the experiences of a whole clan as that of a single person. These tribes again entered Canaan through Shechem, and for a short time lived peaceably with the inhabitants of the land.

Soon, however, wars broke out, as a result of which some of the Hebrew tribes which had settled in the region of the Sea of Chinnereth were overpowered by the Canaanites and others were forced to continue their travels southward, till they reached the Negeb once more.

Israel In Egypt

Disputes among the tribes, represented as the enmity between Joseph and his brothers or between the sons of Leah and the sons of Rachel, again led to the breaking away of some of them in quest of new homes. The bringing of Joseph into Egypt may be the tale of a migration of some of the Bnai Israel to the Nile country, where they successfully established themselves and later invited some of their kinsmen from Canaan to join them. Thus all or several of the Hebrew tribes finally found themselves in Egypt. At first, as shepherds, they were permitted to live their accustomed life freely in special districts assigned to them. Presently a Pharaoh, requiring laborers for his extensive building undertakings and fearing, too, that the Hebrews might join with his enemies in an attack against Egypt, determined to subdue them and to make them slaves of the state. The deliverance of the Bnai Israel from Egyptian slavery marked the birth of the Hebrew nation.

This is the background of our people from which we of today are sprung. Thousands of years separate us from our nomadic ancestors. Since their day we have climbed into the highest places of civilization. We no longer roam the wastes in search of food; nor do we think of all strangers as enemies. In the course of the centuries we have so completely changed that now our ideal is world peace. Let us, then, follow step by step the growth of the nomad or half-nomad into the Jew whom we know today. Our second topic will take us one step forward in our journey and will tell of the birth of the Hebrew nation.

SUPPLEMENTARY WORK

MAP EXERCISES

1. We can always understand our history better if we have some picture in our minds of the places where the events described took place. This section of our text told of our ancestors wandering somewhere between the lands of the great empires of ancient times. Just as we have large countries today, the United States, England, France and Germany, so there were great empires and kingdoms at that time; Egypt, Babylonia, Phoenicia. But while today most of the important nations are located in Europe and North America, at that time they were in Southeastern Europe, Southwestern Asia and Northeastern Africa.

Let us begin by acquainting ourselves with the important kingdoms of antiquity, at least those of which our ancestors knew. On an outline map learn to locate the following countries: Babylonia, Assyria, Phoenicia, Canaan, Egypt, Aram. You should also know the following rivers: Tigris, Euphrates and Nile.

What is the character of the stretch of land east of Canaan and Egypt? What name would suit it best? Write in that name on your map.

2. Are the Oriental empires still important countries today? Do they still bear their ancient names or have changes taken place in them? Study the maps on pages 6 and 7 and see what states these countries now form. Then, on an outline map, name the same places as you did in map one, but if their modern names are different, write their present names.

3. The Bible story relates that our early ancestors came from Ur of the Chaldees or from the city of Haran in the district of Aram Naharaim. It tells that they journeyed to Canaan through Shechem, Beth-El and Hebron to the Negeb. Let us locate these places on an outline map and try to keep their names in mind to see whether they will be important in the future history of Israel.

SUGGESTIONS FOR BIBLE STUDY

Before attempting any Bible reading, you should ask your teacher to show you how to use your Bible. The Bible has an index of its books so that you can find the page on which any book begins. Then learn how to find chapters and verses. Notice the numbers at the top of each page. The heavy black number tells the chapter. The lighter number on the top of the page at the left is the number of the first verse on the page. The one at the right hand top corner tells the last verse on the page.

In the following references, the Roman numbers will show the chapter and the Arabic numbers following will show the verses. Thus XXI 7–10 means Chapter 21, verses 7 to 10. The letter "f" means "and following verse"; "ff" means "and the following verses," that is, you must read as far as you think you will need to, in order to answer any particular question; "p" means page and "pp" means pages.

OUR EARLY ANCESTORS WANDERERS

Genesis XII and XIII describe the wanderings of Abraham's clan or household. These chapters show why the clans wandered and what they carried with them on their march. Notice the difficulties that arise, XIII, 7 to end, when there is insufficient pasture and the clan grows too large.

You will find the same stories, but told more simply, in the *Story of Genesis* by Adele Bildersee, pp. 24–29.

The hard life of the shepherd is described by Jacob in Genesis XXXI, 36–42.

INTERESTING FACTS OF NOMADIC LIFE

Genesis XVIII, 1–10 tells about the homes, separate for men and women, habits of washing, some occupations of men and women, hospitality and habits of eating in the open. Can you find any other facts of interest in this chapter? You may read this chapter also in the *Story of Genesis*, p. 33.

For another tale of hospitality, see Genesis XIX, 1–11, and the *Story of Genesis*, pp. 37–38.

OCCASIONS FOR WARS

Genesis XXVI, 13–22, *Story of Genesis*, pp. 60–61, tells of strife over wells, or

Blood Revenge. Abraham goes to avenge Lot—Genesis XIV. Notice the size of Abraham's army. See how the King of Sodom is willing to divide the spoils, verse 21. See also the *Story of Genesis*, pp. 30–31.

EARLY RELIGION

God appears to Abraham under a tree. Genesis XVIII, 1.

Jacob dreams at the sacred rock or Mazebah at Bethel, Genesis XXVIII, 10–22, and the *Story of Genesis*, pp. 71–73.

A spirit appearing as man fights with Jacob. Genesis XXXII, 23–33, and the *Story of Genesis*, pp. 86–87.

Rachel hides her father's teraphim in her camel saddle. What do you imagine these looked like? You may find some suggestions in the.pictures of this book. Genesis XXXI, 19, 26–35.

The Israelites make a golden calf. Exodus XXXII, 1–6, and Adele Bildersee, *Out of the House of Bondage,* p. 70.

If you are not familiar with the stories of Abraham, Isaac, Jacob and Joseph, read *Story of Genesis,* pp. 24–134 or some book of Bible stories.

QUESTIONS FOR THOUGHT AND DISCUSSION

1. Are we more civilized today than men were in the past? How?
2. Are large nations as a rule more civilized than small nations? Were small nations of ancient times handicapped in ways that no longer are true today?
3. Is it always better to belong to a large group than to a small group; to a large Temple than to a small Temple; to a large society, lodge or fraternity than to a small organization? What are the advantages of either?
4. Are wars as frequent today as they were in nomadic times? What chances has the average man of missing a war during his lifetime?
5. How is war different from a blood feud?
6. How do we today seek justice for injuries? Have we a perfect system of justice or is our justice still unfair in some respects?
7. What substitute do we have today for nomadic hospitality or do we not have any?
8. What are some present day superstitions? Do you believe in any of them yourself? What are some of the things of which you are afraid?
9. Since we no longer believe that God lives in a building, why do we gather to pray at Temples?

10. Why did all ancient peoples practice magic? Why do we not believe in it any more?
11. Why are the stories in the Bible somewhat different from the history told in this book?

ADDITIONAL READINGS

FOR PUPILS

Note: p.=page, pp.=pages, chap.=chapter, chaps.=chapters.

Bonser, Edna M., *How the Early Hebrews Lived and Learned*, pp. 6–32. New York, The Macmillan Co., 1928. (This book tells the history in story form and makes very delightful reading. You may read the entire book through if you wish.)

Powell, E. Alexander, *By Camel and Car to the Peacock Throne*, chaps. IV and V. New York, Garden City Publishing Co., Inc., 1923. (This is the story of travel through Arabia. Skip the hard parts and read the easy ones.)

Hunting, Harold B., *Hebrew Life and Times*, pp. 9–26. New York, The Abingdon Press, 1921. (The book is very simply written and treats the subject somewhat like your text. Several themes, however, are described a little differently, so that you will benefit by reading another account. Mr. Hunting is a Christian and therefore frequently makes statements in praise of his religion, but those have nothing to do with the history of this period.)

FOR TEACHERS

General Introduction to Biblical History

Bailey & Kent, *History of Hebrew Commonwealth*, pp. 1–24. New York, Chas. Scribner's Sons, 1920.

Kent, C. F., *Biblical Geography & History*, pp. 106–114. New York, Chas. Scribner's Sons, 1926.

McCurdy, James Frederick, *History, Prophecy and the Monuments*, Vol. II, pp. 30–77. New York, The Macmillan Co., 1911.

On Nomadic Life

Noyes, Carleton, *The Genius of Israel*, pp. 1–31. New York, Houghton Mifflin Co., 1924. (The most readable single volume on the entire period.)

Bertholet, Alfred, *The History of Hebrew Civilization*, pp. 115–140. New York, Brentano, 1926.

Section II

How Did Our Ancestors Take Their First Step Toward Nationhood?

How Did Our Ancestors Take Their First Step toward Nationhood?

What led them to take the first steps toward becoming a nation?
This section will answer these questions.
It will tell of two great causes which led to the birth of the nation of Israel.
One of these causes was a great event—the going out from Egypt.
We call this event the Exodus.
The second cause was the work of a great man, the greatest Jew of all ages, one of the few truly great men in all history.
The man was Moses.
But how did our ancestors happen to be in Egypt? After they came there, why were they so anxious to escape?
And who was Moses? What manner of man was he to leave such a mighty impress upon the future?
Keep these questions in mind. When you have finished reading this section, you should be able to discuss them intelligently.
Remember the dates for this section.
Israel entered Egypt at about 1350 B.C.E. The Exodus probably took place at about 1220 B.C.E.

How Did Our Ancestors Take Their First Step toward Nationhood?

O UR forefathers, we have seen, began as a number of separate clans, related to each other by language and common ancestry. Yet separate they were, nevertheless, and we have many a story which points to conduct not altogether brotherly. The most famous of these is the story of Joseph, which shows the quarrels among the sons of Jacob.

How did these clans finally unite into one nation? The story of the formation of the union of Israel is long and will require many pages to tell. Here we shall describe only the first steps toward this union. The story may be neither complete nor altogether

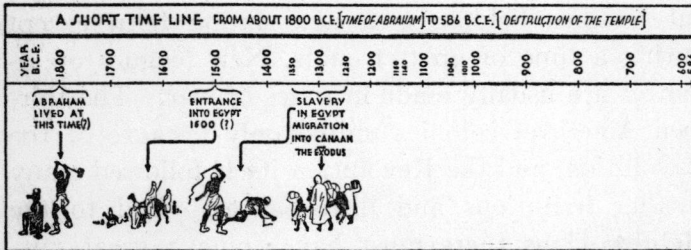

A SHORT TIME LINE FROM ABOUT 1800 B.C.E. [TIME OF ABRAHAM] TO 586 B.C.E. [DESTRUCTION OF THE TEMPLE]

ABRAHAM LIVED AT THIS TIME(?)

ENTRANCE INTO EGYPT 1500 (?)

SLAVERY IN EGYPT MIGRATION INTO CANAAN THE EXODUS

SEMITIC NOMADS SEEK EGYPTIAN HOSPITALITY

Lack of rain often drove desert tribes to seek grazing lands in Egypt as the Hebrews did. This picture is taken from an inscription on the wall of a tomb.

correct, for as we have already pointed out no one truly knows what happened in those early days. Here again our only information is obtained from the stories that were later gathered in the Bible. Reading these stories carefully, we shall select the facts which appear most likely as the real history of our beginnings.

THE EVENT AND THE MAN

People do not, as a rule, change their ways of life unless they are compelled to do so by very powerful reasons. Seldom is a new nation born except during a time of great trouble. New leagues or alliances are usually made in times of war. The thirteen American colonies united only because of the Revolution, and the Revolution itself followed many smaller irritations and disturbances. And to the Hebrew clans there must have come a great misfortune to make it necessary for them to unite.

However, through difficulties alone a people can achieve nothing unless there develops in the mind of some great man a plan of escape from the suffering. A great leader is needed to map out a course of action and guide the people through it successfully. The birth of our Jewish nation is credited to one such man, to our greatest leader and prophet and the greatest religious teacher of mankind, Moses.

The Exodus or Departure from Egypt

The several Hebrew clans, the Bible relates, came to Egypt because of a famine in Canaan. It was not uncommon for shepherd tribes to seek the hospitality of Egypt in years of want, the Egyptian government frequently granting such requests. The rulers of Egypt assigned to the Hebrews the whole or part of the district named Goshen. This land is located in the Delta (the triangular outlet) of the Nile at the northeastern fringe of the Empire. There, although close to the greatest of ancient civilization, the Hebrew clans continued entirely apart from their surroundings in the same manner as they had lived in the desert. The Egyptians, looking down upon shepherds as on persons of lower station than themselves, had few dealings with the Hebrews, who, in their turn, probably never ventured far from their camping grounds into the interior. Thus the lan-

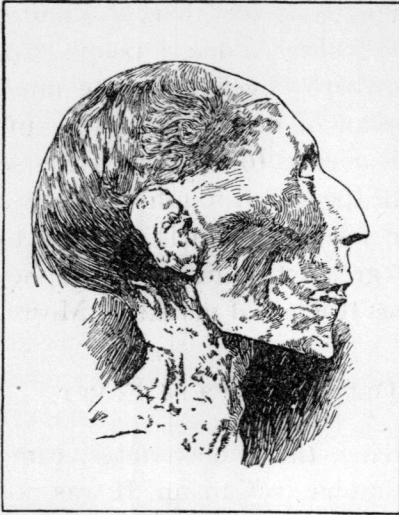

HEAD OF MUMMY OF RAMESES II

It is now in the Cairo Museum and is well preserved. The face still looks like that of a determined man, a strong and vigorous leader.

guage of the clans, their internal government, and laws, their tribal gods, probably even their food and dress continued as they had been in the days of wandering. The Hebrews were still independent desert nomads in all respects except that their tents remained pitched in the same place the entire year, and they must have paid a tax to their Egyptian overlords. The coming of Israel to Egypt took place at about 1350 B.C.E.

Israel Enslaved

Some years after the entry of the Hebrews into Goshen, the armies of Egypt waged war against Canaan and annexed the entire land to Egypt. The following Pharaoh Rameses II, enriched by the tribute which poured into Egypt from the conquered peoples, determined to be a builder rather than a fighter. Many other Egyptian Pharaohs had been famed for their building ventures; but Rameses II wished to outshine them all. He planned to build not palaces or pyramids, but entire cities. To carry out such vast projects in the days before machinery, hundreds of thousands of men were required, to quarry the stone, to haul the enormous blocks, and to lift them into their places. In looking about for laborers the king decided to impress all the foreign clans into service together with his numberless prisoners of war and native Egyptian serfs or slaves. There was special reason for enslaving the Hebrew

GOSHEN
In the Delta of the Nile where Israel lived while in Egypt.

SLAVES AND THEIR DRIVERS
In the days before machinery.

clans, which had come from the neighborhood of
Canaan. Egypt feared an uprising on the part of
the newly conquered Canaanite nations, especially
during a time when the king was occupied with
building work; and it was suspected that, in the
event of war, the Hebrew clans might side with the
Canaanites who were of their own race and language.

Thus the independent Hebrew clans suddenly
found themselves slaves of the Egyptian state. They
were set to building the treasure cities of Pithom

and Rameses. Military overseers were placed over
them to force from them their daily measure of work.
The cruelty of the overseers as well as the slaves'
meager pay are described both in the Bible and in
the stories of ancient Egypt. The stinging whips fell
constantly over bare bodies, sparing neither young
nor old. The days were one round of pain, toil and
fear.

United by Common Hope

Love of freedom, however, was too strongly implanted in our desert ancestors for them to bow

REMAINS OF PITHOM

The picture shows a store-chamber which has been dug out and
uncovered in the site of the ancient city of Pithom in Egypt. This
is one of the places where our forefathers toiled for the Pharaoh.

willingly beneath a taskmaster's rod. There were weaker peoples who might permit their spirits to be broken; but our ancestors never gave up the hope of returning to a free life among the hills where their fathers had camped. Their common suffering only tended to draw the separate clans more closely together. Old quarrels were set aside; old wounds healed; old tales were revived, and new hopes were kindled. All waited for the leader who would free them from their bondage.

Israel Leaves Egypt

The leader did arise, and a favorable opportunity at last presented itself. During a period of severe epidemics, common in Egypt, and while the land was occupied with other inner disturbances, the Hebrew clans, under the leadership of Moses, made a dash for freedom into the desert (about 1220 B.C.E.).

Troubled though the land was, the Pharaoh would not calmly suffer the loss of so many valuable slaves. A detachment of charioteers set out in pursuit. The Hebrews had gone but a short journey from Egypt when they saw behind them the Egyptian spearheads and the tops of their standards. The fugitives, burdened with flocks and families, saw little hope of escape. In despair, they turned upon Moses, prepared to go back and surrender; but Moses ordered them to march on. They forced their children and

THE RED SEA

The water was shallow at this point before the Suez Canal was built. Notice the dike behind which is the canal.

drove their flocks. They were making headway against the Egyptians, when suddenly they saw the sheen of water. In front of them stretched an impassable barrier—the Sea.

The Red Sea

Israel was caught between the Egyptian army and the Red Sea. All hope for freedom, it seemed, must perish forever. A slavery more bitter and oppressive

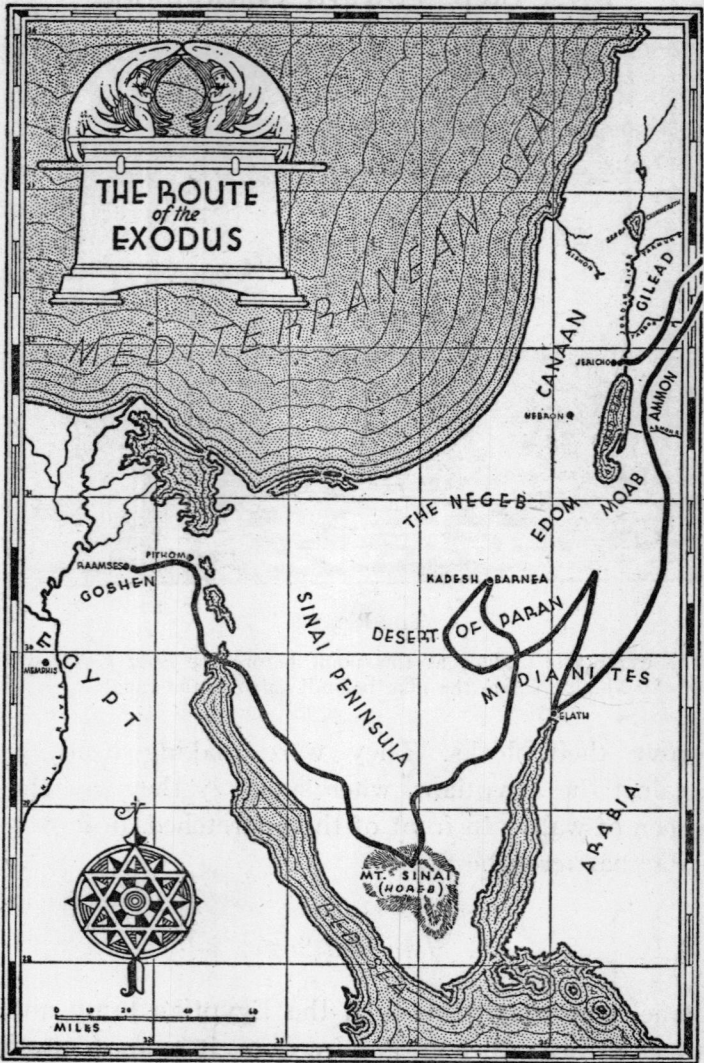

THE ROUTE
of the
EXODUS

MEDITERRANEAN SEA

CANAAN
GILEAD
JERICHO
HEBRON
AMMON
THE NEGEB
EDOM
MOAB
KADESH BARNEA
DESERT OF PARAN
MIDIANITES
ELATH
RAAMSES PITHOM
GOSHEN
SINAI PENINSULA
EGYPT
MEMPHIS
ARABIA
MT. SINAI
(HOREB)
RED SEA

0   10   20   40   60
MILES

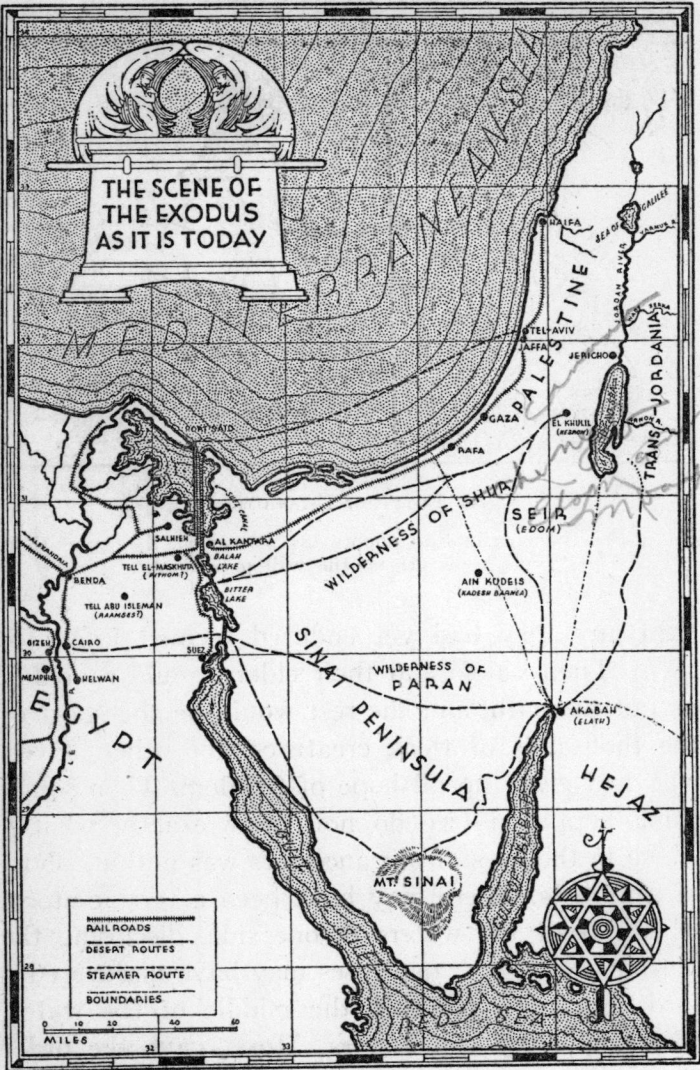

THE SCENE OF THE EXODUS AS IT IS TODAY

MEDITERRANEAN SEA

EGYPT

PALESTINE

TRANS-JORDANIA

PORT SAID

HAIFA

TEL-AVIV

JAFFA

JERICHO

GAZA

EL KHULIL
(HEBRON)

RAFA

SALHIEH

AL KANTARA

BALAH LAKE

TELL EL-MASKHUTA
(PITHOM?)

RITTER LAKE

BENDA

TELL ABU ISLEMAN
(RAAMSES?)

GIZEH

CAIRO

HELWAN

MEMPHIS

SUEZ

WILDERNESS OF SHUA

WILDERNESS OF PARAN

SINAI PENINSULA

SEIR
(EDOM)

AIN KUDEIS
(KADESH BARNEA)

AKABAH
(ELATH)

HEJAZ

MT. SINAI

RED SEA

SEA OF GALILEE

JORDAN RIVER

YARMUK R.

SALT

RAILROADS
DESERT ROUTES
STEAMER ROUTE
BOUNDARIES

0 10 20 40 60
MILES

AN EGYPTIAN CHARIOTEER

He drives the chariot and shoots his arrows at the same time.
From a picture on the wall of a tomb.

than any they had yet endured seemed fated for
them. Their chiefs and their elders would probably
be put to death, and the rest would be the sport of
the thousands of weak creatures, the other slaves,
who had given up all hope of freedom. Then something happened—we do not know exactly what—
which in the eyes of our ancestors was nothing short
of a miracle. There may have been a terrific storm
which swept the waters to one side, disclosing the
bottom of the sea; or Moses may have discovered a
ford, a shallow place in the middle of the water,
where an army could cross. Moses gave the order
to march on, and Israel walked into the sea. With

dry land beneath its feet, Israel strained itself in the race for life and freedom, and succeeded in getting safely across.

The Deliverance

The Egyptians on the farther bank of the sea attempted to cross as the Israelites had done. The reckless drivers rushed their mounts and chariots into the bed of the sea; but to their dismay the Egyptians discovered that their heavy chariot wheels were sinking in the soft mud, and before the chariots could be extricated, the tide began to rise. Those behind, not knowing what was happening, kept pressing on.

Hundreds of chariots were then caught in the middle of the waters, horses and riders drowning, while Israel, from the opposite bank, saw the hand of God upon Egypt.

Never in its later life as a people did Israel forget this deliverance. It always gratefully recalled that it had been freed from Egyptian bondage only through the help of God. "And Israel saw the great work which the Lord did upon the Egyptians, and the people feared the Lord; and they believed in the Lord, and in His servant Moses." [1] The Exodus from Egypt was the great event which gave birth to the Hebrew nation.

[1] Exodus, chap. XIV, v. 31

THE LEADER MOSES

We shall retrace our steps now to the part which the great man, the leader Moses, had in this deliverance. Since Moses is the first great leader about whom we are studying, it might be well to consider for a moment what we mean by a leader.

A leader is a person who teaches his fellow men to be better and to lead a better life. What is a better life? Perhaps this little illustration will make it clear.

When you throw a stone into the water, circles form around it. If you have thrown in a little pebble, few rings will be formed. A large rock will produce many circles, one around the other. Imagine that every one of these circles represents a world or a sort of life which people lead. A person begins in the center and aims to move outward to as wide a circle as possible. The man who is only in the center or in the smallest circles is the savage. He is interested merely in his own family or clan. Every other person in the world is his enemy, with whom he is constantly engaged in fighting. The savage is not very honest or dependable, not because he is mean or unkind, but because, being ignorant and superstitious, he believes that persons of other tribes are lower beings than himself. To this day many people look down upon foreigners, calling them stupid and ignorant, although the foreigners may be as fine and, perhaps, finer than their critics.

When a person learns to respect and understand men of a family or tribe other than his own, he finds himself in a wider circle. His world is now bigger, and he can choose his friends from a larger group. Fighting becomes less frequent, for he discovers that his neighbor has no intention of harming him. That is why we today learn foreign languages, that we may know about all the peoples of the world and live in peace and brotherhood with them. Yet even we are still very far from living in a wide circle. We are still making wars upon other nations as though they were our enemies.

The savage who lives in his narrow circle thinks only of what will be good for his own clan. His acts may be very harmful to other tribes; but that does not concern him. He prays to his god to destroy his enemies in the belief that his god is interested only in his own tribe.

When the savage enters into a wider circle, when he becomes more civilized and his interest reaches out to other groups, he must act so that his conduct will be for the good of all persons in whom he is interested. The savage Indian of Manhattan Island did not hesitate to scalp his enemies who lived in the Mohawk Valley. Today residents of Manhattan and of the Mohawk Valley are fellow citizens of the same state.

Widens World Circle

We may now be able to understand the work of the great leaders. The leaders attempt to draw their fellow men out of their narrow, small world into a wider and better world. The task is difficult because men change very slowly. In spite of all the great leaders who taught us, we are to this day in many respects no better than the men of long ago. You must not be surprised, therefore, to find that frequently after a great leader has passed away, the people appear to have learned nothing from him. Sometimes after a period of years, a nation may even go backwards. Something, however, remains of the leader's teaching. Take yourself as an example. After you have read this book through, you will remember only a small part of what is in it. After a few months or a year, you might not be able to recall anything from it at all. Some few ideas, however, will stay with you. You will find that you know certain facts, though you might forget where you first read them. In the same way the teachings of the leaders lodge themselves in the minds of people who may later forget how the ideas came to them or by whose teachings they are benefiting.

Let us now return to our story and examine the work of Moses and its effect upon our ancestors. In discussing the life and work of any leader, it will help us if we keep in mind the following questions. We have said that a leader aims to make life better than it is. We should, therefore, want to know: (1) What bad conditions did he find? (2) How did he desire to change them? (3) How successful was he?

The conditions which Moses found we have discussed in the first part of this book. Moses set himself the task not only of freeing his brethren from Egyptian bondage, but of leading them out of their narrow circle and ridding them of many practices which were neither fine nor noble. It remains for us to see how Moses hoped to widen this circle, what new life he was planning for Israel, and how successful he was in introducing it.

Let us first learn something about Moses himself.

Early Life of Moses

The early life of Moses is surrounded by legend. You have probably read the Bible story which tells how Moses was saved from the Nile by an Egyptian princess and raised in the palace of the Pharaoh. The story relates that when he was a grown man, in spite of his upbringing in the great Egyptian court, Moses interested himself in his oppressed brothers. Once, seeing an Egyptian beating one of his brother Hebrews, he became so enraged that he killed the Egyptian. The news spread quickly and Moses, fearing for his life, fled beyond the empire of Egypt into the land of Midian. There he was adopted as a member of the household of Heber or Jethro, chief of the Kenites, and was married to one of Jethro's daughters. The Kenites being a shepherd tribe, Moses, too, became a shepherd.

How Moses became the savior of his people is beautifully told in the Bible. The land of Midian lay in the Sinai peninsula, where was located the volcanic Mt. Horeb or Sinai. The frequent flames of fire or columns of smoke which rose from the crater of the mountain led people to believe that it was the home of a great god whom they called *Yahveh* and whom, in accordance with longstanding Jewish custom, we shall hereafter describe by the initial "Y." [1]

Moses Hears the Call

One day while tending his flocks near this sacred mountain, so runs the story, Moses saw a vision which produced a deep effect upon him. A bush had apparently caught fire; yet it did not burn up. It led Moses to think of his brothers in Egypt and of the yoke of slavery which they were forced to bear. If only someone could organize them, he

[1] Yahveh is the correct pronunciation of the Hebrew word which used to be read *Jehovah*. Since we do not pronounce the name of God, we shall merely use the initial *Y*. This practice has been common in Hebrew writings.

thought, and rally them for an attempt at freedom!
Would it be possible to rekindle within them the
desire to be free again and to return to the home of
which they were yearning? And as he pondered, he
felt that perhaps he ought to undertake the freeing

AT THE FOOT OF MOUNT SINAI

Shepherds still graze their sheep at the foot of this mountain of
granite as legend reports Moses to have done hundreds of years
ago. Notice the bare, steep, stony sides of this mountain where
Israel is believed to have received its law.

of his brothers. He saw in this burning bush a call to him to return to Egypt. For a long time he hesitated. He was no orator; indeed, the Bible says of him that he was "slow of speech, and of a slow tongue." He feared that he could not make people believe him or follow him. Yet the call within him was too strong. He parted from his father-in-law, Jethro, and returned to Egypt. There after many difficult labors he succeeded in organizing his brethren for their escape. When the opportunity at last presented itself Moses led his fellow Israelites safely out of Egypt and across the Red Sea.

The Exodus from Egypt marked only the beginning of Moses' labors. Now that the Israelites were safely out of the reach of the Pharaoh, what was to be done next?

Moses Organizes the Israelitish Nation

The Israelites were not yet prepared to advance upon Canaan for the inhabitants of that land were too powerful to be successfully attacked by a host of untrained slaves. Moses feared that if the Israelites were defeated in a war, they would lose courage and return to Egypt. For some time, he thought, it might be best for them to live among friendly tribes, till they could learn to act as one people. He determined, therefore, to lead them to the land where he had been received as a friend upon his flight from

Egypt, and where he had heard the call of God to return to Egypt. During the rest of the life of Moses, the Israelites dwelt among the Kenites in the wilderness of Paran, and in the land known as Kadesh-Barnea, about eleven days journey from Mt. Horeb, or Sinai, the holy mountain.

Having successfully brought his brothers out of Egypt, from slavery into freedom, Moses set about his second task, that of organizing them to live as a free people. The Israelites had always lived in small clans, ruled by the patriarchs. Each clan was an independent group and each patriarch was an

KADESH-BARNEA

A wide plain between hills, strewn with sharp broken rock and scanty grass. Here Israel spent many years on its way from Egypt.

absolute ruler. If they were to unite, the clans would have to give up their independence and the patriarchs surrender their absolute rule. It is the great achievement of Moses that he persuaded these nomadic chiefs to give up some of their powers in favor of union. Thus Moses founded the nation of Israel. Before him there was no nation; there were only tribes which felt in some uncertain way that they were related. Moses strengthened this feeling of kinship till the separate tribes felt that they were brothers. Israel was prepared to move out from its narrow tribal circle into the larger world and into wider interests.

A GOVERNMENT IS FORMED

In their tribal state the Hebrews had had a very simple government. The patriarch was the only officer, acting as general, governor, lawmaker and judge. The patriarch found no need to appoint assistants for any of his work. When the tribes were united, it became impossible for one man to manage all the tasks of government. Further, in order to make the union secure, the various clans had to be given some representation. Moses, therefore, appointed subordinate officers to assist him. The Bible relates that, at the advice of Jethro, Moses chose captains of thousands, hundreds, and tens to perform some of the duties which formerly belonged to

THE DESTRUCTION OF KORAH
As the artist imagined it.

the chiefs. Only the very difficult questions were brought directly to Moses.

Moreover, the Bible tells of a council of seventy elders chosen equally from the various tribes. While we have no record of what this council's work consisted of, we may assume that it was asked to help decide the more important problems of state.

The unification of the people was not secured altogether peacefully and without resistance. We read of instances where ambitious household heads planned revolts against Moses. At one time an outbreak occurred when there was a lack of water, at another time, when food was insufficient. Korah aspired to become high priest, and Dothan and Abiram wished to form a new priesthood. Moses bore these attacks patiently, till his effort finally met with success.

Moses the Teacher of Religion

Even greater than his achievement in uniting the tribes of Israel into one nation and in liberating them from slavery is the work of Moses as a teacher of religion. The religion which Moses taught to a horde of desert nomads more than three thousand years ago is still the foundation for the religions of half the world today.

It may be difficult for us to understand what a difference the teachings of Moses made to our primitive fathers. We have grown up in these ideas, having

never known any others. To us they seem a matter
of course. We must imagine ourselves in the place of
our nomadic ancestors to grasp what changes had to
take place in their lives.

Let us recall what has been said about the nomads' religion. Some nomadic tribes knew of no
gods at all, worshipping merely good and evil spirits.
The tribes which did worship a god thought of him
as belonging to themselves alone. The whole tribe
considered itself as one family of brothers and sis-
ters, and the god was a divine father. As a father,
the god was expected to take an interest in every
tribal undertaking, whether it be a raid on the cattle
of a neighbor or an attack upon a wayfarer to rob
him of his camel and merchandise. When the booty
was divided, the god received his share, just as the
members of the tribe received theirs. They did practice a form of justice, but only within the tribe for
a wrong done to one of their own members, for
their god would be angry if a wrong was not avenged.
Toward other tribes they might act as they pleased,
for their god was not interested in strangers.

BRINGS NEW IDEA OF GOD

Then came Moses with a new notion of God. He
asked Israel to accept a new God, who was the god
not merely of one tribe, but of the whole nation.
This God was far more powerful than any of the

tribal gods whom the Hebrews had worshipped. He
was one of the mighty gods, perhaps the mightiest.
Egypt had been powerless against Him, the Red
Sea divided at His command, and in time He would
also subdue the Canaanites. He had already shown
His interest in the tribes of Israel by leading them

WILDERNESS OF SINAI

In this wilderness of rock, Israel tarried while it received its great
law. Study this picture so that you will understand what a wilderness is. Not all deserts are sandy, as you can see.

safely across the Red Sea. If the Hebrews proved worthy, He would continue to help them and would lead them into the Promised Land.

The old tribal god, who was considered father of the clan, belonged to the clan just as the clan belonged to him. A father must accept his bad children together with the good. The God of Moses did not belong to any single clan. Some of the Hebrew tribes may not have known of Him at all. He was the God who dwelt on Sinai. If Israel wished Y to be its God, it would have to invite Him—it would have to agree to become His people. Just as a foreigner must ask to become a citizen of this country, so Israel had to ask Y to accept it as His people. Israel would have to make promises to Y in return for the protection which it sought. Y would thus become the God of the Hebrews by a covenant or treaty. The Hebrews would have to agree to their share of the covenant, namely, to do the will of their God in return for which Y would adopt them as the people of His choice. If Israel should later fail to live up to its promises, Y could cast it off from being His people. Israel could enjoy the benefits of its God only upon good behavior.

The Ten Commandments

The conditions which the new God set for the tribes of Israel are found in the Ten Commandments.

אנכי ה' / לא תרצה
לא יהי' / לא תנאף
לא תשא / לא תגנב
זכור את / לא תענה
כבד את / לא תחמד

THE TEN COMMANDMENTS

As they are represented in synagogue decoration.

First of all, this God was a jealous God who would share His worship with no other god. The Israelites might still believe that other gods existed; they must, however, worship only *Y*. Nor were they to treat their new God lightly and familiarly as they had treated their spirits and demons. They must neither make any image of Him nor even utter His name unnecessarily. However, it was in their behavior toward their fellows that *Y* was chiefly interested. Do not kill; do not steal; do not bear false witness; do not even desire what does not belong to you. This is the will of *Y*, which Israel must do, if it would be His people.

Thus Moses taught the Hebrew tribes to accept not merely another god, but a different kind of god. Israel could not act toward this God as it had done toward its tribal god. It could not satisfy Him with gifts, because He was master of all that it owned.

This God demanded that it obey His laws which regulated its behavior toward its fellow men. It would have to become mindful of the rights of persons who were in most ways strangers to it. It had left its narrow circle to live in a world which was much greater and wider.

Traces of Magic Are Few

The religion of Moses still clung to some beliefs of an earlier period which later religious teachers were forced to oppose. Thus, in the time of Moses and for centuries thereafter, the Tabernacle was still consulted for the oracle, the will of God being found through the sacred lot, about which we shall read later.[1] The belief in spirits still continued, a story

[1] See page 317

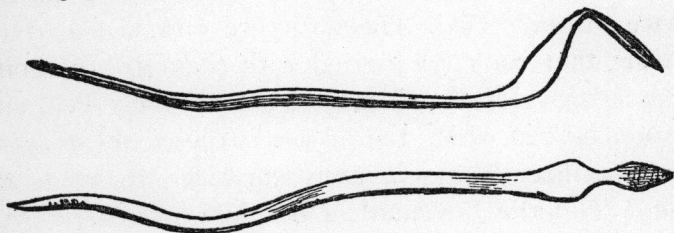

THE BRAZEN SERPENT

The Bible mentions that when the Israelites in the desert were bitten by serpents, Moses set up a brazen serpent in the Tabernacle and thereafter anyone who was bitten looked at the brazen serpent and was cured. Serpents were probably never worshipped as gods but formed a symbol of magic healing among many eastern peoples. The serpents shown in this picture were dug up in excavations in Palestine.

being told how Moses himself was once in danger of his life through the attack of a spirit. Forms of magic were employed even by Moses himself. The Bible tells, for example, that in a battle with the Amalekites, the Hebrews were victorious whenever Moses lifted his hands, and were defeated whenever he lowered them. However, these facts show rather the greatness of the changes which Moses did succeed in bringing about in an age that was so entirely given to superstitions. By comparison with other ancient religions the teachings of Moses were almost free of magic and witchcraft.

WHERE GOD MIGHT BE WORSHIPPED

Some common place of worship was needed toward which all the tribes could look as the dwelling place of their God. The structure had to be of a nature that could be carried with them on all their wanderings. Moses, therefore, set up the "Tent of Assembly," in which the people gathered for prayer and sacrifice. In a separately curtained room stood the Ark of the Covenant, a box in which were two tablets of stone. The Ark served as the symbol of the presence of their God. Wherever the Ark was, there God was supposed to be. Near the tent there was an altar on which sacrifices were offered. Much more than that we do not know about this early sanctuary. In later times there was another sacred tent in which the holy oil and other articles of worship were kept.

The Last Days of Moses

Many years passed before the Hebrew tribes felt prepared to realize their hope of conquering Canaan. Moses was already too old to lead them in this undertaking. He died, the Bible tells, within sight of the promised land for which his entire life was given. His place was taken by his attendant, Joshua, an Ephraimite, who carried the hopes of Moses to successful realization. Israel, however, never forgot its great God-sent leader, its liberator and lawgiver. "And there hath not arisen a prophet since in Israel like unto Moses," says the writer of the Bible.

Moses As We Remember Him

If, then, we should ask again, how did our ancestors take their first steps toward freedom, we should know the answer. Their first step was taken through the Exodus, the going out from Egypt. Above all, however, we owe our beginnings as a civilized nation among the nations of the world to the true father of our people whom our history has chosen to remember as *"Mosheh Rabbenu,"* Moses our Teacher.

In the story of our own or of any other people, no man stands out as great as Moses. No man has entered the life and belief of so large a portion of the world as did this leader of a number of nomadic clans recently enslaved in Egypt. In a half wilderness, a region of bare rocks and fiery volcanoes he taught a law of life which has remained as a seed in the heart of Israel. The seed of a tree planted in the soil will later grow into a trunk with branches, leaves, fragrant blossoms and delicious fruit. The blossoms and the fruit look more lovely than the seed; but their nature is decided by the seed; whatever the seed, so will grow the tree. In like manner Moses planted the seed of our religion. Later generations learned more, understood its meaning better and knew God more fully. This, however, we must always remember, that our people grew as Moses had planted it.

Moses Ranks Alone

We have had many great leaders, teachers, heroes of war, kings, statesmen and prophets who have been recognized by the entire world; but we have never considered anyone in a class with Moses. Moses ranks alone, for he was all that the others were and yet more. Moses began as the great rebel, successfully stirring hopes of freedom in the breasts of slaves. He was the skillful guide and provider in the wilderness, finding food and water in a strange country, building lasting alliances with tribes whose

camping grounds he was obliged to use and eluding
Egyptians and other enemies. Moses was the statesman and leader to whom the tribal chiefs surrendered
their jealous authority. Above all, however, Moses
is remembered as the religious teacher and law giver.
He gave Israel its first constitution, *Torah,* setting
forth how it might conduct itself toward God and
man. To desert men at war with the world he taught
the beginnings of brotherly kindness, justice and respect for the rights of their fellows. In the midst of
superstitions, fear of demons and ghosts of the dead
he taught a religion of trust and courage that was
freer from magic than those of more highly civilized
people. He taught Israel its festivals and Sabbaths.
He gave it its sanctuary, a place of worship without
images. He pointed to Israel the path that would
lead to life in a wider world.

Unchanged by Passage of Years

When you ride on a train, the places you leave behind grow smaller and smaller. The same happens
with men in history. The longer we live, the smaller
and less important do they appear to us. Yet, despite
the passage of thousands of years, the place of Moses
has never grown smaller among us. Later generations
continually discovered new qualities of greatness in
him. Four books of the Bible tell the story of his
life and teachings. Endless legend has continued its

weaving of tales about him, to our own day when books still reverently record his deeds.

When we read the Bible story and all that has been written thereafter, we feel that we know Moses closely. We can see him, a tall powerful bronzed man, already old when he enters upon his great work. We picture him sitting at the entrance of his tent, throughout the long hot day, listening patiently to complaints, great or small. All seek his judgment, because they know his unbending fairness. When necessary, he can put aside his robe of justice and take up the weapons of war. He is then the stern warrior, fighting back his people's enemies. He may have to punish treason among the backsliders in his camp. Yet in his heart he so loves his people that he would gladly have given his life in exchange for their safety. Nor is he

Michelangelo

MOSES

jealous of others who exercise authority that should
be his. "Eldad and Medad are prophecying in the
camp," his servant Joshua reports; but Moses replies
that he wishes all of God's people were prophets.
Despite all his greatness, history knows him as the
most modest of men. He lived simply and died so
that "no man knoweth of his sepulchre unto this
day," in the words of the Bible.

Therefore, when the great sculptor, Michelangelo,
dreamed of carving the figure of Moses in stone, he
thought of Moses as a man who was greater than
man.

IMPORTANCE OF THE EXODUS TO ISRAEL

The Israelites have always looked back upon the
Exodus as the greatest event in their history. The
Exodus to them was the Birth of their Nation. The
whole future of Israel had been in the balance. It
was either to be free or else lose itself in Egyptian
slavery, a fate suffered by so many other races and
tribes which had fallen under the power of Egypt.
The commemoration of the great event was made
part of the observance of all our festivals, particularly of the Passover. The Bible tells us that anyone who fails to participate in this great festival shall
be cut off from his people.

The Exodus is important to us as the birthday of
our religion, which was declared in the wilderness

of Paran. As we celebrate the birthdays of great men, so in an even greater measure does the birthday of our religion deserve our fond thought.

Above all, the Exodus is important to Israel because the memory of it was forever used as a warning and a lesson. The people of Israel must never become oppressors, since they themselves had been oppressed in the land of Egypt. Repeatedly the Bible commands, "Ye shall not oppress the stranger, for ye know the heart of the stranger since ye were strangers in the land of Egypt"; "Remember that ye were slaves in the land of Egypt—therefore I command you to help your poor, etc."

History is full of examples of peoples who have not learned through their own experiences. Too frequently a nation which has gained its freedom after years of dependence becomes in its turn an oppressor of others. Many subject nations in Europe which were given their independence after the Great War have already forgotten their own suffering and are treating the people who are dependent upon them more harshly than they were treated themselves. It is, therefore, with great pride that we look back upon our forefathers who never permitted themselves to forget that they, too, had once been strangers in Egypt.

To this day we have daily reminders of our Egyptian slavery in our morning and evening prayers and in the grace after meals. The experience of our slavery has taught us to come to the help of the weak and the oppressed, and to champion the rights of human beings everywhere.

AND A STRANGER SHALT THOU NOT WRONG, NEITHER SHALT THOU OPPRESS HIM; FOR YE WERE STRANGERS IN THE LAND OF EGYPT. EXODUS 22:20

SUPPLEMENTARY WORK

Map Exercises

1. The district through which Israel traveled after it left Egypt is one of the least familiar spots in the world today. It is almost entirely desert with no permanent settlements, still largely traversed by caravans, although a railroad was recently built through it, between Egypt and Palestine. Even the places which are mentioned in our early history can no longer be located with certainty. Geographers of the region have attempted guesses about some of the locations which we have placed on the map, on page 76. We shall therefore ask you to become familiar with only a few places. On an outline map showing the lands of the Exodus, locate the following: Egypt, the Nile, Goshen, Sinai, Kadesh-Barnea, Gulf of Suez, Red Sea, Persian Gulf.

We should know where these places are in relation to Palestine. Let us therefore also locate Canaan, Philistia, Ammon, Moab, Edom, Phoenicia, Aram.

2. There are several places about the Sinai Peninsula which are important today for two reasons other than those related to our early history. One reason is the Suez Canal providing a short route by water between the Mediterranean and the Indian Ocean through the Red Sea. The second important fact about that region today is the railroad which connects Egypt to Palestine, making possible our ancestors' forty years' journey in about ten hours. As a result of the railroad and canal, new and different places are the important centres today. Let us learn some of these on our outline map. Locate Cairo,

104

Alexandria, the Suez Canal, and Port Said. Also draw a line to show the railroad. You will find the information on the map on page 77.

Suggestions for Bible Study

The story of which this section tells forms one of the most beautiful portions of the Bible. You may read the story in a specially selected children's Bible.

Out of the House of Bondage, by Adele Bildersee, pp. 1–78, 103–106, 115–124, 157–160.

Questions for Thought and Discussion

1. Is there any reason why we wish to remember and be proud of the fact that our ancestors were slaves in Egypt?
2. We said that one of the reasons for our considering Moses great is because he united the separate tribes. How do we feel today toward strange nations? List ten nations in the order in which you like them, the best liked first and the least liked last. After you have made your list, compare it with that of your classmates and discuss the reasons for your choice in class. Is your reason based on knowledge or prejudice?
3. Is it proper in war time to pray to God that He should harm our enemies?
4. What ought the Passover remind us of in regard to the treatment of other persons and nations? What can we do about it as citizens of the United States?
5. What difference does it make whether God is thought of as moral or not? Do we act today as though we believed all the nations children of one God? Give examples.

6. How does the United States treat strangers? In which ways is it kind to them? In which ways is it unkind?

ADDITIONAL READINGS

FOR PUPILS

Note: *op. cit.* means that the title of the book was given in an earlier section, f.=page following, ff.=pages following.

Hunting, *op. cit.*, pp. 28–30.

Dubnow, S. M., *Outline of Jewish History,* Vol. I, pp. 51–91. New York, Max N. Maisel, 1925. A history by a famous historian, perhaps a little hard, but it will help you to get a further understanding of this period.

Bonser, *op. cit.*, pp. 125–190.

"Passover of Long Ago," *The Young Judaean,* Vol. XIII, April, 1924, p. 2 ff. New York.

Fram, Rabbi Leon, "Lincoln and Moses," *Young Israel,* Vol. XVI, Feb., 1924, p. 6 f. Cincinnati.

Alexander, Cecil F., "The Burial of Moses," *Poems for Young Judaeans,* pp. 57–58.

Benton, Rita, "Up, Up from Egypt,"—A Play—*Shorter Bible Plays,* pp. 53–61. New York, The Abingdon Press, 1922.

(Fiction)—Canfield, W. W., *The Sign Above the Door,* Philadelphia, The Jewish Publication Society of America, 1912. An exciting but imaginary tale of Egypt during the plagues.

Kamman, Morris, "The Boy Moses," *Young Israel,* Vol. XX, May, 1928, pp. 8–9; June, 1928, pp. 12–14; July, 1928, pp. 8–11.

FOR TEACHERS

Noyes, *op. cit.*, pp. 32–71.

Bailey & Kent, *op. cit.*, pp. 25–46.

Kent, *op. cit.*, pp. 115–123.

McCurdy, *op. cit.*, Vol. II, pp. 78–105.

Margolis & Marx, *A History of the Jewish People*, pp. 14–21. Philadelphia, The Jewish Publication Society of America, 1927,

Section III

What Kind of Land
Was Canaan?

Israel Is Headed for Canaan.

We told of that in the previous section.
But what sort of land is Canaan?
Is it a fertile country where men can gain a livelihood through agriculture?
Is it level or hilly? Has it springs and rivers?
Is it a country easy to conquer but as easy to lose or is it hard to win but easy to defend later?
Does the land receive sufficient rainfall? Is the weather pleasant?
These and many more questions would be in the minds of the invading Israelites.
These facts will have great importance for the future history of Israel.
Study the geography of Canaan carefully. Study particularly the maps given in this section as well as the picture map inside of the book covers.
Then close your eyes and see if you have a picture of the land in your mind.

What Kind of Land
Was Canaan?

THE nomadic tribes of Israel were now united under one God. For many years they remained at Kadesh-Barnea, until this union was made strong and lasting. At last they were ready for the next step in becoming a real nation—that of getting a land for themselves.

There was one spot toward which they turned, the land of Canaan, where they remembered their ancestors had pastured their flocks. From their parched desert the distant green mountain tops of Canaan looked, indeed, like a land of promise.

Nevertheless, when the time arrived for undertaking the conquest of the country, the people grew a little afraid. They wanted to be certain about the nature of the land and the difficulties which they might expect to meet. Accordingly, we are told in the Bible, men were sent to spy out the land. The Bible relates the instructions which Moses gave to the spies: "Get you up there into the South and go up into the mountains; and see the land, what it is; and the people that dwelleth therein, whether they are strong or weak, whether they are few or many; and what the land is that they dwell in, whether it

is good or bad; and what cities they are that they
dwell in, whether in camps, or in strongholds; and
what the land is, whether it is fat or lean, whether
there is wood therein or not. And be ye of good courage and bring of the fruit of the land." [1]

Two Questions

The instructions given to the spies show the questions which troubled the people: What kind of land
was Canaan, and how easily might a people gain its
livelihood there?   Above all, they wondered whether
Canaan could be successfully conquered. They desired to know whether the inhabitants were strong or
weak, how exposed the country was to attack, and
how invaders might hope to keep supplied with water and food. We can thus restate the purpose of the
spies' mission as being to find out, first, whether the
land was worth conquering and, secondly, whether
the land could successfully be conquered by the
Hebrews.

Was Canaan Worth Conquering?

Would the spies find Canaan worth conquering? Let
us take an imaginary tour of the land with them and
see what they would find upon inspection. We shall
start with them from Kadesh-Barnea, a half desert

[1] Numbers, XIII, 17

region south of Palestine, and proceed northward. Let us follow the map so that we shall know where we are going. You will find the map in pictures on the inside cover of the book.[1]

We Enter Mountain Country

North of Kadesh-Barnea we enter the Negeb, which means the south country and also the dry land. As you may guess from the name, the Negeb is a district which receives little rainfall and is, therefore, only slightly better than the desert. Even the Negeb might appeal to us better than Kadesh, but the truly desirable country still lies before us. A mountain range rises, steep, rugged and very rocky. This is the beginning of a range running north and south through the entire country and known as the Central Range. We begin our climb which is to carry us to a height of almost 3,000 feet above sea level. We are already in a region where men can live a settled life. True, the soil on the mountain sides is thin and rather poor, and the valleys between the mountains narrow, often rocky and, therefore, difficult to cultivate; but we feel that we are in fertile land, no longer in the desert. The climate, too, is temperate and comfortable. Many pleasant sights ease our hard ascent. The

[1] According to the Bible story the spies probably did not go as far into the country, as we have described. We are telling only what would have been seen if a trip had been taken through the land of Canaan at that time.

THE MOUNTAINS OF JUDAH

Steep, rugged and very close together. This land is fit only for
grazing.

stony mountain side is broken like a staircase of
platforms. Each platform is fenced about with stones
so that rains might not wash down the thin soil. We
call such fenced platforms, terraces. They are planted
with vines; the clusters of grapes grow large and
luscious in the warm sun. We also see many olive
trees which seem to grow between the rocks. Herds
of sheep and goats find enough grass to nibble and
manage to keep a foothold on the slippery stone.

WE PASS CITIES AND HAMLETS

Along the road are numerous hamlets of small
mud huts. Tents are rarely seen, though we do pass

occasional caves which serve as dwellings. In this land people live in homes, real houses that shelter them from sun and cold.

There are larger settlements, cities with walls and towers, built on the summits of the hills. We head toward them, taking the wide road and mingling with men on foot or on donkeys. Soon we pass through the gate and find ourselves in the market place, where we look upon the displays of strange articles which we know only wealthy farmers can afford. We are afraid to explore the city too far and, therefore,

CAVES

In these giant rocks there are large, deep caves which have often served as homes for poor people, or places of hiding for outlaws. This picture shows the caves near Tiberias in Galilee. There are similar caves in other parts of the Central Range, particularly in Judah.

REHOBOTH

A flourishing Jewish settlement located in the Southern mountains, later called the Mountains of Judea.

merely examine the walls and gates and return to the open country again.

We are near the top of the mountains, which we find to be plateau or table-land, fit for cultivation. Here are crops of barley and millet, the poorer of the grains, but good for food nevertheless.

An Inviting Plain to the West

From our high position we can look about us for miles on all sides. On the extreme west lies a great sea. Between us and the sea is a plain, broad at the southern end and narrowing as it proceeds northward. That is the Coastal Plain. We send a party down to inspect it. Our messengers descend the steep mountains and find themselves in a range of lower hills called the *Shephela*, or low land. At last they are on the plain, later to be known as the Land of the Philistines. The land is the choicest they have yet seen. Rich fields of wheat and corn spread southward down the plain, which widens from 12 to 40 miles. Fruit and nut trees, fig palms, pomegranates and citrons are seen everywhere. The climate is rather hot; but the sea breezes and the trees afford relief. Wide roads cut through the plain, the main highways over which the caravans pass from distant

TEL AVIV

This is a new city settled by Jews who have returned to Palestine in recent years. Tel Aviv is located on the Mediterranean Sea, just north of Jaffa. In ancient times the site was probably the northern border of Philistia or immediately above it.

MOUNT CARMEL

Which shuts off the Plain of Sharon from Phoenicia. Today, at
the foot of Mt. Carmel, lies the flourishing city of Haifa which
is soon to become the principal port of Palestine.

Mesopotamia and Phoenicia on their way to Egypt.
The plain is dotted with cities, large cities where the
great caravans stop to rest and trade. One or two
cities are on the sea, and their harbors are filled with
ships rowed by strong bronzed slaves to the seaports
of the Nile and Mediterranean. The wealth of these
cities, their palaces, the robes of their important citizens and the equipment of their soldiery form the
themes of our conversations for many days.

The Great Oak Forest

North of this region the plain narrows and is covered with a great oak forest. The forest reaches as

far as we can see, till it climbs up Mount Carmel, which extends into the sea. This region is called the Plains of Sharon. We explore it somewhat, following the wide, well-worn and busy caravan roads. The land here rises and falls in low hills. We pass many little rivers and frequent marsh land, showing that there is much water under the soil. We pass some sand dunes, too, formed by sands which the winds have brought in from the sea. Everywhere there are beautiful flowers, millions of them, as far as the eye can see—lilies, roses, poppies and other colorful varieties.

We Return to Camp

We shy at the thought of having to climb up the steep mountains again. The wide roads lead straight on past Mount Carmel. Fortunately, our packs are light. We know, too, that our friends above are expecting us.

We are advised that it would be more comfortable to travel either northward up to Mount Carmel where we could pass through the Valley of Dothan, and then turn south into the mountains by good roads which the merchants and soldiers use, or we could go south through the Negeb and then up the road that we had taken from Kadesh. Being good climbers, we take the steep paths to our fellow-spies who are waiting for us.

A Deep Valley and a Great Sea on the East

Another party sets out for the great sea at our right. This party soon finds itself upon the edge of a mountain which descends almost as a straight smooth wall of stone thousands of feet to the sea below. The mountain wall is, indeed, over 4,000 feet to the bottom where the Dead Sea flows, flanked by a similar wall on the opposite shore. The land about the sea and about the part of river which is near the sea seems to be a wilderness; rain never falls there and the heat is tropical. Our company lingers long enough to find out that the sea, known in early times as the Salt Sea and today called the Dead Sea, is the end of a very deep valley through which flows the Jordan River.

Something strange happened to the earth in this part of the world thousands of years ago. The earth's surface cracked, forming a deep ditch sloping downward to a depth of about thirteen hundred feet below sea level at the Dead Sea. The river which flows through this valley is, therefore, called in Hebrew *Yarden* which means the descender. The Dead Sea itself, a body of water 47 miles long and between three and nine miles wide, is shut in on all sides. Its water cannot flow off anywhere, and, therefore when the sun carries off much of it by evaporation, all the solid minerals contained in the water remain

VIEW OF THE JORDAN

Notice the steep sloping sides and rich vegetation.

JERUSALEM

Just outside the city walls.

in the sea. The waters are, therefore, said to be so heavy that a person cannot sink in them.[1]

Jerusalem

Our party returns and we continue northward through the mountains. A large city lies in our path, in the highest part of the mountains. The city, called Jerusalem, is built on sheer rock, and the mighty walls and towers which rise about it on all sides look like a part of the mountain itself. We admire

[1] Recently a Jewish company was formed to extract the valuable minerals from the Dead Sea.

A VALLEY IN SAMARIA

The picture shows one of the beautiful, wide valleys in the district
north of Jerusalem. At a later time the famous city of Samaria
was located here, giving its name to the entire district.

the great stronghold and are a little fearful of entering it. We stand outside of its gates for a while, enjoying the crowds, and buy a few small articles and some food at stalls which are set up outside of the gates.

Pleasanter Mountain Land

We resume our journey northward and having traveled about forty miles from the Negeb, we enter narrow passes between steep hills which lead us out of this range into a new district. This region, also, is mountainous; but the hills are neither as high nor as rugged as those which we have passed. The valleys between the mountains are wide and fertile. We come upon fields of wheat and barley, extensive vegetable gardens, large vineyards, and orchards of all sorts. Herds of large cattle graze in the meadows. Milk is so plentiful that the land is said to be flowing with it. Throughout the countryside busy farmers follow their oxen yoked to their plows. We see people everywhere, more than in the southern range. We also see more homes, more trees, more villages, and many more cities. On the high roads we frequently pass caravans. How jolly life must be here in contrast with the loneliness of the desert! What rich spoils such a country could afford!

We can still see the plain on the west coast as far as the peak of Mount Carmel. On the east, the river

EIN CHAROD IN JEZREEL

Modern machinery was brought to Palestine by recent settlers. This flourishing district was for many years permitted to become a dangerous swamp, a breeding place for malaria. Recently Jewish workers drained it and made it a garden spot.

valley is no longer desert, but full of rich vegetation. At one point it widens into a large plain about fourteen miles wide, where we see the flourishing city of Jericho, set in a forest of date palms extending several miles. Somewhat to the north the valley narrows and is overgrown with wild tree and bush. We are warned that lions, wild boar, bears and foxes live in the jungle by the river banks.

Out of the Mountains

We proceed about forty miles further north. The hills become lower and end abruptly at the foot of the Plain of Jezreel. The plain is shaped like a tri-

THE PLAIN OF JEZREEL

The prize land of ancient Canaan. Many flourishing Jewish
colonies are located there today. The Hebrew word for valley
is "Emek" and this region is therefore referred to as the "Emek."

angle widening from west to east. Through it flows
a river called Kishon. At its western tip a narrow
strip connects this plain with the upper coastal plain.
We follow the valley eastward for over twenty miles
till a number of broad terraces finally lead it down
to the Jordan Valley. The Valley of Jezreel, later
called Esdraelon, seems the most fertile district that
we have yet passed. The cities about it are perched
in the mountains at the edges of the valley. The
valley itself is like an extensive field of golden wheat.
Everywhere the land is in bloom. Our only complaint
is that this section, like other plains and valleys, is
very warm.

More Mountains and Another Great Lake

We proceed northward further across the valley.
Again we ascend a mountain range which rises in
gentle hills and wide valleys. At the head of the
Jordan we see a large lake which, we learn, is called
Chinnereth, the Harp, and sometimes also the Sea of
Galilee, because the land about it is known as Lower
Galilee.

This section is as pleasant and almost as fertile
as the plain. The hills are well wooded with bush
and tree. Everywhere we hear the rushing of mountain streams. About the shores of the lake are
cities and large flourishing farms. Trade routes to
every section of the eastern world turn in through

ON BEAUTIFUL CHINNERETH

The city of Tiberias in Galilee is located on the shores of the lake.

this district. We watch the passing caravans and strain after them as long as we can hear the tinkling of the camel bells.

We Cross the Jordan

Before returning we decide to visit East Jordan, whose high straight mountains line the eastern banks of the river. Passing through the torrid Jordan Valley and climbing about 2,800 feet above the bed of the river, we come upon a plateau which rolls on as far as we can see into the vast Arabian desert. From our position there is no sign of desert, for the fertile region stretches between thirty to eighty miles eastward.

We had noticed at least three large rivers that flowed into the Jordan. We now see one of these, the Yarmuk, fed by numerous springs and rivulets, which, together with its tributaries, is as large as the Jordan itself.[1] We find that the other rivers, the Arnon and the Jabbok, also have water all the year round. The land is, therefore, rich in grass and trees, in part having even excellent soil for wheat. The climate, as in the western range, is temperate, and while on the west the tropical Jordan Valley lies below us, on the north Mount Hermon rises snowcapped during the entire year.

[1] Where the Yarmuk falls into the Jordan the power of the falls is being employed by the Ruttenberg Company today to generate electricity for Palestine.

The district of Gilead immediately to the south of
the Sea of Chinnereth is rich in valuable spices and
healing herbs. The entire east Jordan, we are told, is
rich pasture land where many thousands of oxen,
camels, sheep and donkeys graze from one year's
end to the other.

THE MOUNTAINS OF GILEAD

These mountains rise steep and tall to a table-land which rolls off
into the distant desert. Notice the many trees and thick bush on
the mountain side.

TOPOGRAPHICAL
MAP of
PALESTINE

MEDITERRANEAN SEA

COASTAL PLAIN

CENTRAL RANGE

SEA OF CHINNERETH

PLAIN OF JEZREEL

JORDAN VALLEY

DEAD SEA

EAST JORDAN PLATEAU

	BELOW SEA LEVEL
	S.L. TO 600 FT.
	600 " 1500 "
	1500 " 3000 "
	ABOVE 3000 "

A SUMMARY REPORT

We are all quite enthusiastic over the country and should certainly wish to possess it. We prepare a diagram in the form of a map, to enable us to report clearly what we have seen, to the rest of the camp.

The entire country, we estimate, is about 150 miles long and from 40 to 80 miles wide at various points. The most important part of the country seems to be the Central Range running north and south, but broken into by the Plain of Jezreel. On the west between the mountain range and the sea lies the Coastal Plain. East of the Central Range is the sunken Jordan Valley with Lake Chinnereth at its northern end and the Dead Sea at the south. Beyond the Jordan rises the table-land of East Jordan, a mountain range that may have been part of the Central Range before the earth cracked to form the Jordan Valley.

Rainfall and Seasons

Before returning we inquire about the rainfall. In a warm country like Palestine, we are told, the valleys near the sea and the mountain regions which are cool receive most of the rain and are, therefore, fertile. The rain clouds ascending from the Mediterranean Sea water the Coastal Plain and then rise

over the Central Range. The cool mountain air forces
the clouds to contract, and so we have violent rains.
Past the mountains the clouds travel over the Jordan Valley which, as we have seen, is below sea level,
from 680 feet at Chinnereth to 1,300 at the Dead
Sea. The higher you ascend, the cooler it becomes;
the lower you descend, the hotter it is. The heat of
the Jordan Valley, especially in the lower portion,
expands the clouds so that rain seldom falls there.
Across the Jordan there is another stretch of high-
land. The clouds once more rise into a cooler region
and give up their rain. Gradually the clouds spread

DESERT OF JUDAH

Winds and storms have worn these craggy summits smooth.

out as far as they can, and where they no longer reach the desert sets in.

Palestine has two seasons, one dry and the other rainy. The rainy season itself comes in two parts, the early rains commencing in October or November and lasting till January or February, and the latter rains coming as heavy showers in March and April. During the wet season there are heavy rainfalls filling up the rivers and streamlets. In the rainless season, however, most of these streams dry up and only a few rivers such as the Jordan, Yarmuk, Jabbok and Arnon contain water all year. Natural springs are more abundant in the north of Palestine than in the south.

Is Canaan Worth Conquering?—The Answer

You will recall that we had set out to learn whether Canaan was worth conquering. Our answer, as you may guess, would certainly be "Yes." The land could satisfy every need which the nomadic Hebrew clans might have. Except for one small region, the land is quite fertile. While the country is not large, it offers a choice of all manner of soil, natural features and climates. There is farm land, grazing land, orchards, mountains, plains, valleys, hot climate, temperate and cool sections. Although the territory occupies less than 10,000 square miles, no more than one of our small states such as New Hampshire, it was spacious enough for the nomadic clans. Indeed, the Bible relates that thirty-one independent little states made their home in Canaan at the time of the Hebrew invasion. There would be sufficient water from rain, springs and rivers; there were trees, homes and cities. The Bible even suggests that there were iron and copper there, though we no longer find any today.[1]

The Sections We Like Best

Thus on our return journey we discuss, in earnest or jokingly, in what part of the country each of us would like to settle.[2] Some will have nothing less than the Coastal Plain with its broad fields and orchards. Short of that they may take Jezreel. Others complain that the plains are too hot—they would rather settle somewhere in the Central Range. They insist on Lower Galilee or the portion below Jezreel, which was soon to become the Mountains of Ephraim, or the district of Samaria. Others have been attracted by East Jordan. Gilead, they insist, is their first choice. There they could watch their flocks while they themselves lay lazily under a shady oak all day. Some of us confess we would be content even with the southernmost portion of the Central Range, the

[1] Deut., chap. VIII, v. 9

[2] You probably know that many Jews have settled in Palestine during the last forty years. Many of these Jews are now farmers. Examine the map of Modern Palestine and see where the Jewish colonies are located. Did the ancient Hebrew clans occupy the same district? Bear this question in mind when we study the next section.

district through which we passed first. (That section was later to become famous as Judah.) Nobody seems to care for the Jordan Valley. Jestingly we divide among ourselves the houses, fields, trees, cattle and sheep. We shall let the Canaanites work for us. They will be our slaves and we shall be the masters. We decide to bring some samples of the land's fruits to our waiting brethren.

CAN THE LAND BE CONQUERED?

However, we were to bring back a report not only whether the land was worth conquering, but whether the Israelites would be able to conquer it. On our

THE MOUNTAINS OF EPHRAIM

journey northward we had permitted ourselves to enjoy the pleasant sights as though the country were already ours. Now we must prepare to give advice that may spell the success or failure, the life or death of the future of our people.

From which direction shall we advise the Hebrew tribes to advance against Canaan, and at what point? Some are for marching due north from Kadesh-Barnea, up the southern section of the Central Range. There are some objections: any climb for purposes of attack is dangerous; the enemy has all the advantage of higher position and familiar land; besides, should the Hebrews succeed and reach as far as Jerusalem, they would certainly be stopped there; the city which commanded the passes seemed like a huge smooth wall of stone.

Others advise marching eastward and then north through East Jordan. East Jordan, they assert, is a land easy to enter and to occupy, for it possesses few fortified cities; but what shall be done after East Jordan is taken? At what point shall the Jordan be crossed? Some advise crossing at Jericho. Others protest they could never take the city with its tremendous walls. They might enter through Jezreel where there are few fortified cities; but, it is pointed out that in the plain, the Canaanites will be able to use their horses and chariots against our men on foot. The mountain regions, on the other hand, presented the difficulty of strongly fortified cities which could not be stormed without battering rams, scaling ladders and other machinery.

We can thus readily understand the biblical account telling that the spies returned discouraged, declaring that the Hebrews were unequal to the difficult task of conquest.

Natural Aids and Hindrances

Some among our party would undoubtedly point out that the very nature of the land was in our favor. Mountains, valleys and plains divide the country into little districts like a checkerboard. Each section is so separated from every other that each forms a small independent kingdom at war with its neighbors. Often the kingdom consisted of no more than one city with its surrounding fields and villages. We have already mentioned that the Bible lists thirty-one such little city states at the time of the conquest. Some of us, therefore, believe that a large united army could easily overcome each of the little kingdoms separately.

The majority are afraid. They pass by nations whose names and military fame have often been repeated in our camp with fear. The Amorite lived here, as well as the Canaanite, Hittite, Jebusite and Amalekite, to mention only the most outstanding among them.

Would the Hebrews be able to conquer the land

of Canaan? Should they break in through the mountains or through the plains? Should they attempt passing through the Coastal Plain? How successful would the conquest be? That will be the theme of our next section.

SUPPLEMENTARY WORK

Map Exercises

1. So much of the history of our early ancestors is bound up with Palestine or the Land of Canaan, particularly with its surface features, that we must know the land well to appreciate our history fully. The mountains of Judah and Ephraim, the Vale of Esdraelon, the pasture land of Gilead or the Plain of Sharon, each had its effects on shaping the fortunes of our forefathers. Let us therefore become acquainted with the geography of the land, with its main divisions or zones, so that when we speak of events happening at various points, we may be able to place them in our mind immediately. On an outline map let us do the following:

Draw heavy black lines running from North to South that will divide the country into its main zones, namely, the Coastal Plain, the Central Range, the Jordan Valley and the Eastern Plateau.

Draw dotted lines from East to West that will show the Negeb, Edom, Moab, Ammon, Galilee, Judah, the Philistine Plain, the District of Samaria, the Valley of Jezreel, the Plain of Sharon and Galilee. Show high mountains by X, somewhat lower mountains by △ and low hills by O.

Locate also Gaza, Beer Sheeba, Jerusalem, Shechem, Jaffa, Carmel, Damascus, and Tyre. We shall use these and a few more places as the key places. If you know these places, you will be able to locate any other point in Palestine by saying that it is North, East, South, or West of one of the key cities.

2. Which parts of Canaan would fall to the share of our ancestors? Would they conquer the good rich land or would

140

they succeed only in getting grazing country and thus be little better off than in the desert? Let us make a fertility map of Canaan, and when we read the next section, let us try to recall the regions and see which fell to the share of Israel.

On an outline map let us do the following:

Shade all desert sections red.
Shade least fertile regions gray or black.
Shade fair grazing country yellow.
Shade fairly good farm land blue.
Shade the best land green.

Use the description in the text, the picture map inside of the book covers and particularly the map on page 131 in your text. You will also find help in Bailey & Kent, History of the Hebrew Commonwealth, map No. 2, page 397.

Locate again all the places that were suggested for map No. 1. See how many of the key names you can already write down from memory.

SUGGESTIONS FOR BIBLE STUDY

After you have read this section, you should be able to follow the story of the spies as told in the Bible and to understand why the spies reported as they did. Read either Numbers XIII, XIV, 1–10, or The Twelve Spies in *Out of the House of Bondage*, pp. 107–114.

What later generations of Israelites thought of their land after they were already settled in it is described in the following passage, Deuteronomy VIII, 7–10.

QUESTIONS FOR THOUGHT AND DISCUSSION

1. Is Palestine today a good country in which to live? Is it worth spending large sums of money to colonize Jews there?

2. In what section of Palestine would we buy land today? Where are the most flourishing Jewish colonies actually located?

3. If the Jewish Agency sent persons to explore Palestine today, what favorable and what unfavorable reports would they bring back?

4. Do nations still acquire new lands by conquest as they did long ago? Think back of the past fifty years. You might get some help from your history teacher in public school.

5. What report would you have brought back if you were one of the spies? Why?

ADDITIONAL READINGS

FOR PUPILS

Kussy, Sarah, "Palestine, Old and New," *The Young Judaean,* Vol. XV, December, 1925, pp. 14 ff.

Coffin, Helen L., "A Bible Interpreter," *Young Israel,* Vol. XXI. Oct., 1928, pp. 12–13. This article shows how our American Southwest helps us to understand the geography of Palestine because both sections are so alike in many ways.

Feuerlicht, Ethel M., "Palestine the Beautiful," *The Young Judaean,* Vol. XIII, Dec., 1923, pp. 14 ff.

Phillips, Rev. A. L., *The Geography of Palestine.* Richmond, Va., Presbyterian Committee on Publications, 1904.

Moses, Regina, "The Romance of the Emek," *The Young Judaean,* Vol. XVI, January, 1926, pp. 11 ff.

FOR TEACHERS

Smith, George Adam, *Historical Geography of the Holy Land.*

George H. Doran Co. Select what you wish from the volume. This book is the standard authority.

Bailey & Kent, *op. cit.*, pp. 47–59.

Kent, *op. cit.*, pp. 3–84.

Bertholet, *op. cit.*, pp. 11–30.

Margolis & Marx, *op. cit.*, pp. 4–13.

Section IV

How Did Conquest of Canaan Help Our Ancestors Become a United Nation?

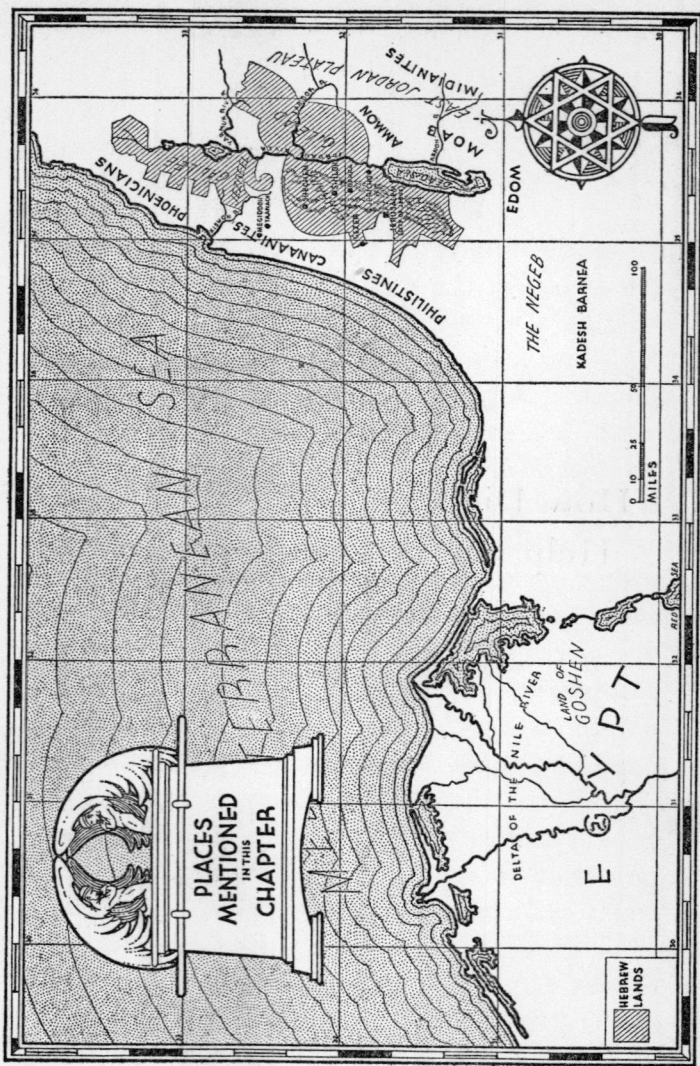

PLACES MENTIONED IN THIS CHAPTER

MEDITERRANEAN SEA

PHOENICIANS

CANAANITES

GIBEON
HAMOTH

JORDAN PLATEAU

EAST

AMMON

MOAB

MIDIANITES

PHILISTINES

EDOM

THE NEGEB

KADESH BARNEA

EGYPT

DELTA OF THE NILE RIVER

LAND OF GOSHEN

RED SEA

MILES
0 10 25   50   100

HEBREW LANDS

How Did Israel Become Master of Canaan?

From which direction would the conquest begin?
*The spies were not at all agreed. How do you
imagine they would advance against the land?
Make your guess and then read what really did
happen.*
*The text will also tell of grave dangers or crises
through which Israel passed during the early days
in Canaan.*
At first Canaan was only partly conquered. *Many
strong cities defied the Israelitish advance for
many years.*
*Groups of tribes were left to win and to hold their
possessions as best they could. Each group was
obliged to act for itself.* There were thus four
small Israelitish nations instead of one.
*You may well imagine what happened. Enemies
quickly took advantage of the division and almost
succeeded in wresting the land from Israel, as
Israel had conquered it from the Canaanites.*
But the dangers themselves united our ancestors.
Fortunately, too, champions arose, called judges,
who led their brothers successfully through these
wars.

*The dangers or crises which almost destroyed Israel
turned out to be a force for good. They led to the
formation of a unified nation of Israel.*

Who were these leaders and what was the nature of
the crises?

This section will tell about them.

*Remember the dates for this period. The Conquest
began at about 1180 B.C.E. This period lasted till
about 1100 B.C.E.*

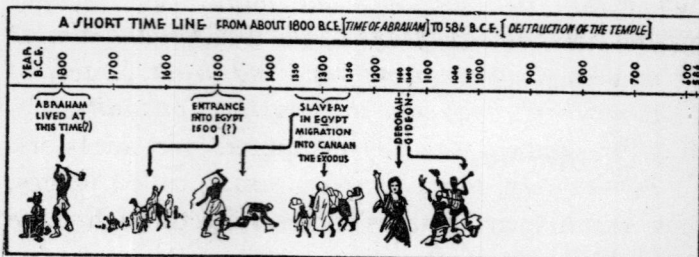

A SHORT TIME LINE FROM ABOUT 1800 B.C.E. [TIME OF ABRAHAM] TO 586 B.C.E. [DESTRUCTION OF THE TEMPLE]

How Did Conquest of Canaan
Help Our Ancestors Become
a United Nation?

A T the close of the last section we saw how difficult a task the conquest of Canaan would prove for desert people. We know that Canaan later became the land of Israel; but how rapidly and under what conditions did the Israelites succeed in conquering the country? Did they conquer all of it, or only a part? Were they obliged to make compromises with the inhabitants of the land?

Above all, since we are interested in following the growth of our ancestors into a nation, we are curious to learn how the conquest affected them. Did it help them to become a nation more rapidly or did it, on the contrary, delay their growth? In order to answer this question, let us see how the conquest occurred. We may then see what results it produced.

How Was Canaan Conquered?

Look carefully at your map and try to figure out from which side the Israelites would begin their invasion of Canaan. The stories about the conquest are uncertain. We do not know exactly from which side the attack began; and most likely the Israelites moved against the land from several points. Some writers even assert that the Hebrew tribes in Galilee and in the Negeb had never left for Egypt, but had continued in Canaan. Since the facts are not altogether definite, our maps may be of help to us.

Invasion from the South

The Israelites, you will recall, were encamped at Kadesh-Barnea, south of Canaan. Evidently the simplest way for them to proceed against Canaan would have been to march northward through the Negeb, up to the lower part of the Central Range. The Bible tells of an attack made from that direction which was repulsed. However, the attack may have proven partly successful. It is likely that the tribe of Judah, joined by the Kenites and Kenizzites, clans which inhabited Kadesh-Barnea, attacked the inhabitants of the Negeb and succeeded in forcing their way as far north as Hebron. The southern portion of the Central Range thus became known as the Mountains of Judah.

Attack on East Jordan

The majority of the Israelites, however, particularly the Joseph tribes, Ephraim and Manasseh, did not

HEBRON TODAY

Hebron is one of the oldest cities in Southern Palestine. In the Bible, Abraham is reported to have purchased a burial cave here for his wife, Sarah, and later David was crowned king of Judah at this place. Today Hebron has become associated with a massacre by Arabs against Jewish talmudical students during the riots of August, 1929.

move upon Canaan from the south. They chose to go by way of the east and then up the easy slopes of the Eastern Plateau. East Jordan, as we saw, was not fortified and, therefore, was unprepared to withstand such a huge invasion.

The southern part of the Eastern Plateau was inhabited by tribes against which the Israelites either feared or did not care to wage war, because they considered them as related to themselves. These were Edom on the far south, and Moab and Ammon

EDOM

Located in a half wilderness, south of the Dead Sea. This picture shows the site of the city of Petra meaning the "Rock." You can easily understand why the city received this name.

on the east.[1] The invasion began above the river Jabbok, in the land which is marked Gilead on the map. Though settled by two kingdoms, this coun-

[1] In accordance with the Bible story, Edom is called the brother of Jacob. Ammon and Moab are described as sons of Lot, the nephew of Abraham. This means that the founders of these peoples may at one time have belonged to one clan, dividing when the clan became too large.

try seems to have fallen an easy prey to the Israelitish armies.

The excellent pastures of Gilead afforded a resting place for the Hebrew tribes. They remained there for some time, during which Moses died and Joshua, of the tribe of Ephraim, was chosen their leader. Since Gilead was insufficient for all the tribes, they

A SCENE IN MOAB

Moab was to be Israel's southeastern neighbor. Its population was engaged in cattle raising. This picture shows a group of its present day inhabitants sitting about a well.

decided to cross the Jordan. The tribes of Reuben and Gad, the Bible tells us, made East Jordan their home on the condition that they would serve as the vanguard for the remainder of the conquest. The other tribes used this region as a base for further attack against the Westland.

The Jordan Crossed—Occupation of Central Highlands (About 1180 B.C.E.)

The main body of the Israelites headed by the tribe of Ephraim and under the leadership of Joshua, crossed the Jordan at Jericho. In a strange way, by some stratagem, the great walls of Jericho fell before the invaders, who destroyed the city completely as an offering to *Y.* They then proceeded against the middle of the Central Range. The road leading into this part of the mountains is not a difficult one. The mountains, as we have seen, are not very steep, and there are wide valleys between them. The greater part of this territory, consisting of open fields and small villages, fell into the hands of the invaders. There were, however, many fortified cities which were too strong for the poorly armed Israelites. Thus, for many years the open country was held by the Israelites while the walled cities such as Shechem, Gezer, Taanah or Megiddo, some in the center of the district and some on the edge of the Plain of Jezreel remained under Canaanite rule. The Israelites

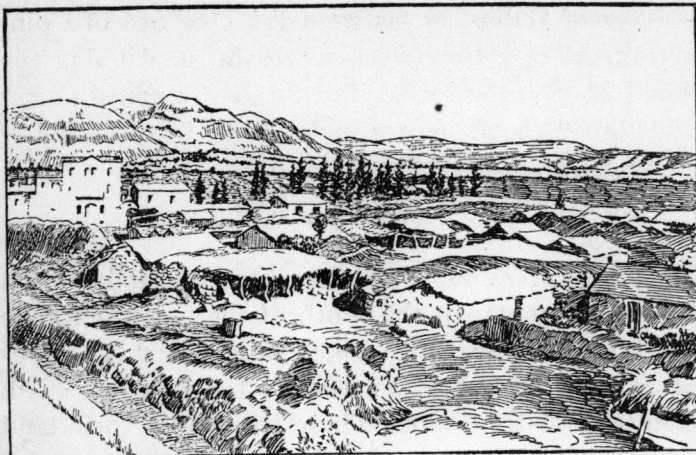

JERICHO TODAY

In olden times Jericho was an important and strongly fortified city set in a palm forest. Today it is a small Arab village. The land around it is still rich in vegetation as you can see from this picture.

who settled in the middle section of the Central Range were known as the descendants of Rachel, namely, the tribes of Ephraim, Manasseh and Benjamin. Later the tribe of Manasseh found itself too crowded in its territory and a part of it returned to settle across the Jordan. You will thus often find the Bible speaking of half the tribe of Manasseh.

Success in Galilee

Another group of tribes, Issachar, Zebulun, Naphtali and Asher, pushed northward into the section around the Sea of Galilee or, as we call it, the Sea of Chinnereth. At first they were successful in winning the land but soon the former inhabitants regained power and forced the Israelites under them in servitude.

EXTENT OF EARLY CONQUEST

The early invasion of the Israelites resulted thus in four settlements. In the south of the Central Range lived the Judaeans, with whom were joined the tribes of Simeon and Dan, as well as the non-Israelitish Kenites and Kenizzites. These tribes won their land after a desperate struggle which lasted many years. The central highlands were settled by the Ephraimites and the tribes related to them, namely, the tribes of Manasseh and Benjamin. They held the open country and made headway slowly against the Canaanites of the cities. The tribes in the Northern Highlands near the Sea of Chinnereth, having first conquered the country, were later reconquered by the Ca-

A CANAANITE CHARIOT

The chariot was a small fighting wagon drawn by two and later by more horses. The Canaanite chariots, which the Israelites later introduced, were manned by three soldiers. One was the driver, a second the fighter and the third protected the other two with his shield.

naanites. The settlement in Gilead, east of the Jordan, appears to have been the first to become thoroughly Israelitish.

Important Cities Still Unconquered

Some of the most important parts of Canaan were still in the hands of the Canaanites. The Coastal Plain, the avenue of the main trade routes, never became Israelitish territory. The Plain of Jezreel, too, surrounded by strongly fortified cities, resisted the early Hebrew invasion. The Canaanites enjoyed the superior advantages of iron chariots which the Hebrew footmen were unable to oppose on the level plains. In the mountain districts, too, as we have seen, there were many fortified cities which for a time successfully maintained their independence. One section of the land must be particularly pointed out, that lying between the territories of Ephraim and Judah. The strip of land in which the city of Jerusalem is located, the highest and steepest part of the Central Range, was inhabited by a people called the Jebusites, who held out against the Israelites for several hundred years. Not till the days of King David was the land finally brought under Hebrew dominion.

The unconquered Canaanite regions had important effects upon the Hebrew tribes, cutting one section off from the other. Thus Ephraim was cut off

WHERE JEWS ARE
SETTLED IN
MODERN PALESTINE
(SHADED AREAS ON MAP)

MEDITERRANEAN

SYRIA

DAMASCUS

METULA

ACRE (ACCO)
HAIFA
Mt. Carmel
NAHALAL
AFULEH
EN CHAROD
TIBERIAS
SEA OF
GALILEE
(CHINNERETH)
DEGANIA
RUTTENBERG WORKS

NABLUS
(SHECHEM)
Samaria

PETAH TIKVA
TEL-AVIV
JAFFA
RISHON LE ZION
REHOVOTH

JERUSALEM

Judah

TRANS-JORDANIA

RUHAMA
GAZA

SINAI PEN.

RAIL ROADS
ROADS
DRIVING ROADS
STEAMER ROUTES
BOUNDARIES

MILES
0   5   10   20   30

so effectively from Judah by the Jebusites that each section developed as a separate people for several centuries. The Plain of Esdraelon separated Ephraim from the tribes in the north, while the hot Jordan Valley and the Jordan River divided the Westland from the East. Each of these four settlements was, therefore, forced to live by itself and, taken up with its own troubles, had little time or thought for the other tribes. It seemed as if the union achieved in the days of Moses was in danger of being destroyed.

RESULTS OF THE EARLY CONQUEST—BENEFITS

Was the conquest of benefit to the Israelites, or was it harmful? Without doubt we should say that it was of great benefit to them. Acquisition of a homeland marked the change of the Israelites from a nomadic or partly nomadic people to settled nation. This is a most important change in the history of a people. As nomads the Israelites would forever have remained in a very low state of civilization. As a settled people they could move forward to higher stages of progress.

We may readily imagine the benefits which Israel would derive from settled life as contrasted with a life of wandering. Settled peoples are certain of their food and enjoy a much more ample supply than do nomads. Their lives are, therefore, more comfortable and, as a rule, more peaceful, for they no longer need to resort to raids in order to obtain food. Their whole manner of life, their occupations, their morals, and their laws, undergo a change. We shall describe these changed conditions in a later section.

THE WATER RESERVOIR AT GEZER

The Canaanites were already highly civilized when the Hebrews appeared. We know it from the many remains which have recently been dug up. This picture shows a well-constructed reservoir for the collection of water at the city of Gezer which is located in the Shephela.

THE DISADVANTAGES—THE BREAKING UP OF THE UNION

There were other results which were hardly pleasant or beneficial. Many bad consequences came together with the good. We have noted before how in the course of the conquest each group of tribes sought out its own territory and became separated from the others by natural barriers as well as by absorption in its own problems. As a result, the feeling of brotherhood and kinship, the sense of belonging to one common family, began to weaken. The teachings of Moses, which had barely been implanted in the hearts of the people, were soon forgotten. Strife among the tribes again became frequent, old blood feuds were renewed, and former ideas of right and wrong and the thought of one's own tribe as the enemy of all other tribes were revived.

Imitation of Canaanitish Worship

A difficulty even more serious than the breaking up of the tribes into distinct sections soon faced the Israelites. As desert men they were unfamiliar with the arts of settled life. Each new occupation and skill had to be learned from the Canaanites. If the Israelite wished to know how and when to plow, when to plant, how to trim a vine or olive tree, how

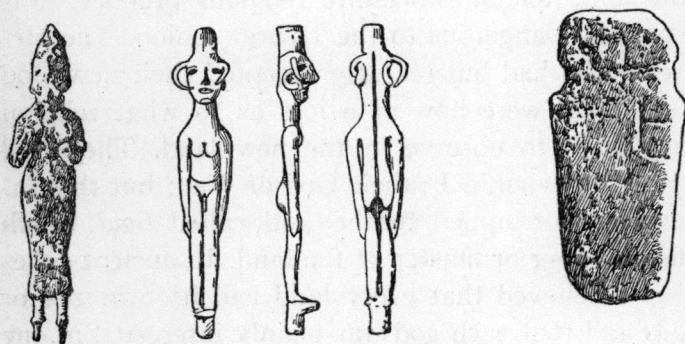

HOUSEHOLD GODS

These idols were found at Jericho, Taanach and Gezer. The first at the left shows an Astarte in bronze. The next three figures also in bronze show Astarte with horns, a form commonly used by the Babylonians. At first Baal may have been worshipped merely through a stone or *Mazebah*. Here you may notice the attempt to cut a face in the flat rock.

to build a house or mend a tool, he was obliged
to depend upon the native Canaanite as his teacher.
The Israelite was thus bound to regard the Canaanite as his superior. The Canaanites already knew the
art of writing and possessed a written literature.
They were skilled builders of fortifications, temples
and palaces. The Canaanite merchants traded with
every part of the civilized world. It was natural that
the Hebrews should admire Canaanite modes and
practices and attempt to imitate them in the handicrafts, the arts, and even in religion.

CONSIDERED A PART OF AGRICULTURE

The imitation of Canaanite religious practices was
especially dangerous to the Hebrew union. The Hebrews who had but recently accepted their new God
Y at Sinai were now at a loss as to what religion
they were to observe in the new land. They still
wished to worship Y, their God of War; but the Canaanites worshipped another god, called *Baal*, which
means owner or master of the land. In ancient times
people believed that every land had its own god or
gods and that each god was mainly interested in one
branch of human activity. One god was believed to
care chiefly for the needs of the farmer, another for
the soldier, a third for the hunter, and so forth.
Baalim were mainly farmer gods, whose blessing the
Canaanites believed, were needed for the success of

the crops. At all stages of farm work, therefore, it was important to please the god. You probably have observed how pious people today recite a prayer over their food and drink, at rising and before going to bed. The Canaanites had their religious ceremonies or rites before every agricultural undertaking. There would be prayers for rain, special ceremonies at plowing and planting, magic rites to bring later rains and good harvests. The Canaanites would insist that farm work could not be done without all these religious observances. If any were omitted or performed improperly, the crop would surely result in failure.

There were other occasions, too, when the Canaanites prayed to their gods. If any ailment occurred, if a person died or if a pestilence broke out, the Canaanites insisted that the gods of the land were angry. The superstitious Canaanites would assemble on their high places or in the glens of the forest to offer up prayers and sacrifices to the gods. No gift was too costly to offer up to the angry gods and to the evil spirits. There appears proof that at times they offered up their own children as sacrifices.

WEAKENS HEBREW UNION

The equally superstitious Israelites were not slow to follow their example. They, too, became eager to make their peace with the gods and spirits which

AN OLD CANAANITE HIGH PLACE

Notice all the sacred stones. Sometimes they were arranged singly and sometimes they were placed in a circle as you see in this picture.

owned the land. Like the Canaanites they began to employ the magic prayers as did the Canaanites. Soon they, too, were worshipping the gods of the land, the *Baalim,* in addition to the God whom they had brought with them from the desert. Even the worship of their own God Y was changed to resemble that of the Canaanites. Each group followed the example of the district in which it was settled; and, since the Canaanites differed among themselves in their gods and religion, the Hebrews did likewise. The teachings of Moses were thus giving way to more common heathen worship. The strongest bond of union, namely, the worship of one God, was gradually being loosened.

The Period of the Judges—Movements Toward Union

Had nothing occurred to change this condition, our ancestors might have broken up into separate clans once more, or formed little kingdoms by mingling with the surrounding Canaanites. We today might have been among the Fellahin or Arab peasants who inhabit Palestine. We should then have said, in answer to the question of this section, the conquest of Canaan hindered rather than helped our ancestors in becoming a nation. Fortunately, many causes roused our ancestors to new efforts. Powerful enemies attacked them, who could be met only by a union of all tribes. Within their own ranks, too, strong leaders arose, known as the Judges, who in periods of distress rallied Israel about the common standard of their wilderness God.

Let us consider the dangers which threatened the new settlements and the Judges who arose to save their people.

The Final Struggle with Canaan

Who owned the land, the Canaanites or the Israelites? That was to be settled in a last great contest.

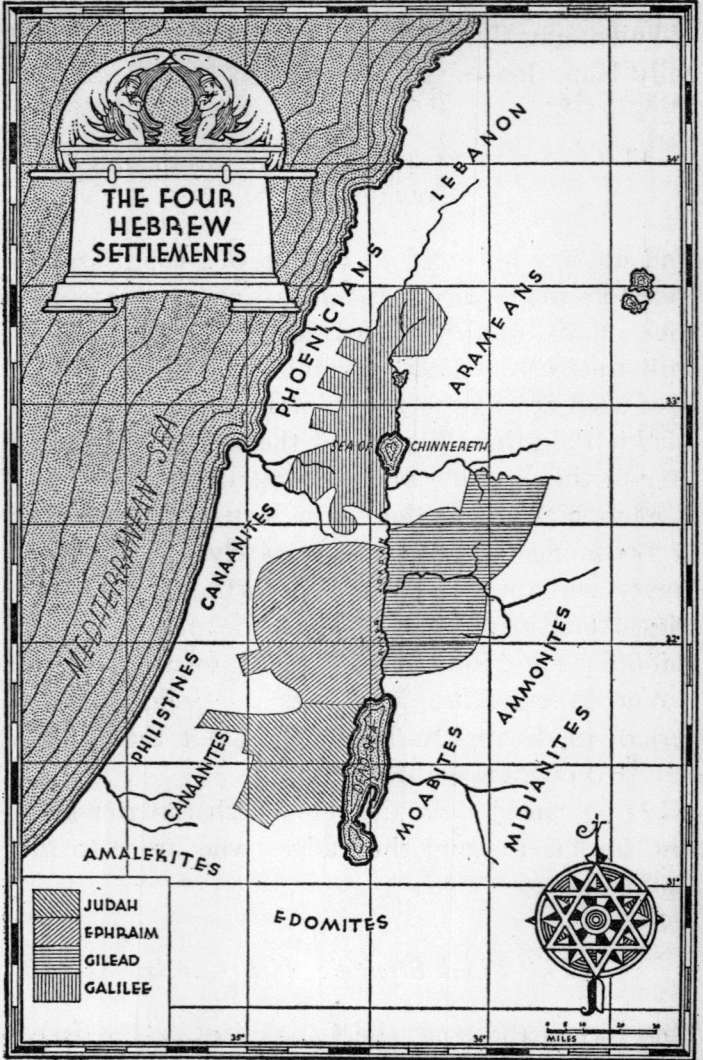

THE FOUR HEBREW SETTLEMENTS

LEBANON

PHOENICIANS

ARAMEANS

MEDITERRANEAN SEA

SEA OF CHINNERETH

CANAANITES

PHILISTINES

CANAANITES

MOABITES

AMMONITES

MIDIANITES

AMALEKITES

EDOMITES

JUDAH
EPHRAIM
GILEAD
GALILEE

MILES

Thus far, as we have seen, neither side could claim mastery. In the Central Range Ephraim was slowly gaining the upper hand; but the tribes of the North were under the yoke of the Canaanites. The large Plain of Esdraelon, which separated Ephraim from the northern tribes, was completely in Canaanitish hands. The Canaanite kings, realizing that their defeat was due to disunion, decided to form a confederacy of all their forces to overwhelm the Hebrews. A final battle was to be fought out in which one or the other had to win decisively.

The Canaanite attack found the Hebrews poorly prepared. The Ephraimite tribes alone could not hope to withstand the combined armies of Canaan. In the meantime, the Canaanites seized the caravan roads, interrupted travel and communication, and kept the peasants in terror. In many villages the population was disarmed, and Canaanitish supremacy seemed assured.

THE JUDGE DEBORAH

Fortunately a leader was found who guided Israel through this crisis. The leader was a woman by the name of Deborah, famed as a priestess or prophetess who had her shrine under a sacred tree in the hill country of Ephraim. Her shrine was the center of worship of Israel's own God, Y, the God of Moses. Y was still worshipped with fear even by those who added *Baalim* of the land to the number of their gods. Many pilgrims visited her shrine to seek the word of God, to offer gifts, or to have their quarrels judged. They came from all parts of the land, from every tribe and from every village, for they looked upon Deborah as the chief priestess, the holiest representative of their national God.

Deborah felt that she was the only one who could call all Israel to the banner of their God, the God of War; but there were many obstacles in her way. Her chief difficulty was that she was a woman, for no man would join an army led by a woman. The Israelitish soldiers would be ashamed to admit that there was no man among them brave enough to lead them to battle. Besides, the Israelites were poorly armed and had no iron chariots with which to meet the Canaanites in the plain. Deborah, however, trusted to the spirit of the people and looked forward to the aid of God, which she was certain would be forthcoming.

THE BATTLE AT JEZREEL

Deborah selected one of the chieftains of Issachar, Barak, the son of Abinoam, to be the leader of the hosts of Israel. Then she issued a call to arms to all the tribes of Israel. Their common danger forced tribal jealousies aside. Mindful of the strength which had been theirs during their early union, large num-

THE BROOK KISHON

In the Valley of Jezreel. The brook overflowed its banks at the time Deborah fought the Canaanites. Their iron chariots became useless on the muddy plain and they were defeated.

bers answered the summons and gathered at Taanach, in the Valley of Jezreel. There a mighty Canaanite army, heavily supported with chariots and under the leadership of Sisera, prepared to meet them.

In the engagement which followed, exceptional good fortune favored the Israelites. The battle was fought in the early Spring, after the heavy rains. There had been unusual rainfall, which made the battlefield soft and marshy. Adding to the difficulties of the Canaanites, the brook Kishon, swollen by the rains, overflowed its banks and made of the land a large swamp on either side. In a swamp the heavy armor and chariots were but a hindrance. The chariot wheels sunk into the mud, imprisoning their riders and exposing them to the lightly armed Israelites. The Hebrews thus won a decisive victory. The Canaanite power was now completely destroyed, not only in the Mountains of Ephraim, but also in Esdraelon and Galilee. The Canaanites never recovered from their defeat and remained Israel's bondsmen.

After the Crisis—The People Forget

There was great rejoicing after the victory. The exploits of Deborah and Barak were remembered in a famous song that was written to commemorate the event.[1] The God of Israel once more proved himself the most powerful of gods.

The people returned to their homes, and in the quiet pursuit of their occupations forgot the danger which had recently threatened them. Again each section and each village became occupied in its own problems, giving no thought to the common needs. Deborah died, and no great priest or seer took her place. The earlier wars had not resulted in any fixed plan of united action for future wars. When, therefore, a new danger befell the land, the tribes of Israel were as unprepared as they had been for the former crisis. Before they could even take counsel,

[1] Judges, chap. V

their best lands were overrun, and many were obliged
to hide in caves and caverns to save their lives.

The Conflict with Midian—The Judge Gideon

The new enemy consisted of a group of nomadic
tribes, called Midianites, who came from the region
of Kadesh-Barnea, the land where Israel had once
lived. They followed the same route as Israel had
taken perhaps fifty or a hundred years before. Ar-

MIDIANITES

Typical Bedouins as we can still see them today.

AN ANCIENT ALTAR

Legend used to gather about these ancient stones, often connecting them
with the fathers of the Jewish people.
This is the sort of stone which Jacob
might have declared a holy place, in
the Bible story of Jacob's dream at
Beth-El.

riving in Canaan at harvest time, when the crops were to be gathered, these hordes easily overcame the feeble resistance of the separate tribes. They overran the choicest lands, those of Ephraim and the Plain of Esdraelon, disarmed the population, and prepared to carry away all the fruits of the year's labor.

Yet whenever danger threatened, a brave man usually came forth in defense of his people. And when the leader or judge did appear, he knew there was but one way to gather the divided tribes under one standard, namely, to call upon them in the name of their own God. The leader in this new crisis was Gideon of the tribe of Manasseh.

DESTROYS ALTAR OF BAAL

Gideon's first act aroused the anger of his fellow villagers against him. In his native home of Ophra, as in all other villages of Manasseh and Ephraim, stood an altar for the worship of the Baal of the land. Gideon knew that so long as each section worshipped its own Baal, it would remain disunited and deliverance would not come to Israel. In the quiet of night Gideon, with the assistance of his friends, pulled down the altar of Baal and destroyed it. The Asherah, or sacred tree, which stood near it was cut down and burned. Only a heap of broken stone and ashes remained of the Baal's place of worship.

When the superstitious villagers awoke in the morning and saw what had been done, there was a great commotion among them. An assembly quickly gathered and demanded that those guilty of the crime be punished with death. Gideon's wise father saved his son's life. "What fools you all are," he called to the people, "that you should fight the battle of your god. If Baal has in truth any power over Israel, let him avenge his own

GIDEON'S FOUNTAIN

This spring is believed to be the one where Gideon led his army to test their endurance. Only three hundred did not break ranks, and with these Gideon proceeded against the Midianites.

wrongs, for has not my son destroyed his altar? If he cannot avenge himself, why should you fight his battles?"

The Israelites soon came to regard Gideon as the leader in this period of danger. Young men gathered about him, till his army numbered ten thousand men. The Midianites heard of the Israelite preparations but troubled themselves little over it, feeling vastly superior in numbers.

TESTS METTLE OF HIS FOLLOWERS

The victory of Gideon over the Midianites is related very vividly in the Bible. Gideon knew that he could not meet the Midianites in open battle and, therefore, determined upon a night surprise. Only the bravest men could be trusted for this undertaking, and Gideon accordingly determined to test his army. After a hot day's march, he led the men past a stream. The parched soldiers, without the permission of their chief, fell quickly to the cool sparkling water; but Gideon marched on, taking no notice of the water, and a handful of men followed his example. When the whole army had passed the stream, the number of those men who had not knelt to drink was found to be three hundred.

With these three hundred men Gideon planned a surprise attack upon the enemy. That night, while the camp of the Midianites was asleep and unguarded, Gideon gave each man a horn and a pitcher containing a torch. They were to enter the camp of the enemy quietly, spread among the tents, and do as their leader would do.

VICTORIOUS OVER MIDIAN

These directions were very carefully followed. When all was ready, Gideon smashed his pitcher against the tent poles, set fire to the tent with his torch, and blew upon his horn as though he were calling upon a regiment to charge. Three hundred pitchers instantly smashed, tents were aflame, and three hundred horns seemed to call upon as many regiments. The sleeping Midianites were terrified. In the great confusion their thought was only of flight. The remainder of Gideon's army now joined the battle and pursued the Midianites to the Jordan, where they slew many who attempted to cross. Gideon himself set out in pursuit of the Midianite chiefs who were responsible for the death of the members of his own family. According to the laws of blood revenge, Gideon felt it his duty to avenge his murdered relatives. Thus ended the invasion of the Midianites, and Israel was saved again.

The success of Gideon showed that, disunited though the Hebrews were, a great danger might bring them together under a leader who called them in the name of their God. Yet even at such a time all tribal jealousies were not forgotten. The old clan feeling was still so strong among some of the villages that, when Gideon was pursuing the fleeing Midianites over the hot plain, many villages refused food to his tired and hungry soldiers. After the battle the tribesmen of Ephraim threatened Gideon

WHERE IDOLS ONCE STOOD

In these nooks or crypts cut out of rock idols once stood. These crypts are now found in many parts of Palestine. Often travelers follow a well-worn trail only to find it ending at some such ancient high place.

for not having invited them to lead the attack. Only his mild reply prevented a civil war.

FIRST ATTEMPT AT FORMING A KINGDOM

The Israelites were unwilling to let this opportunity pass again without planning for some common action in the future. The wisest plan, it seemed, was to choose a king over all the tribes. The one person who might rightfully claim the honor was Gideon. Gideon did not quite wish to accept the kingship, though he seems to have lived in kingly fashion. He

hoped to preserve the spirit of union by setting up
a golden image at his home, thus making of Ophra
a royal sanctuary, and one of the important centers
of worship for Israel.

When Gideon died, one of his sons, Abimelech,
born to him by a Canaanitish wife from the city of
Shechem, decided to accept the dignity which his
father had refused. With the help of Canaanitish followers he proclaimed himself king of Shechem and
for three years he maintained his kingdom over the
mountains of Ephraim. Abimelech's cruel slaughter
of the other members of the family of Gideon, as
well as the fact that he was only a half-Israelite,
turned the people against him. The old spirit of dis-
sension broke out, with no immediate outside danger
to quiet it. Abimelech, too, did not properly worship
Y, the God of Israel, but was a follower of the god
Baal Brith of Shechem. The people rose in rebellion,
as a result of which the city of Shechem was be-
sieged and completely destroyed by Abimelech; but
while attacking the nearby city of Thebez, a woman
standing on the wall threw a millstone upon the
king's head and killed him. In this manner ended
the first attempt at kingship in Israel.

Further Signs of Union—Shiloh

While the attempt at union through kingship had
failed, one force was yet at work which drew the

tribes of Israel a little closer together, namely, the worship of *Y*. *Y* was believed to dwell in the Ark of the Covenant in which were kept the two sacred stone tablets brought from the desert. Wherever, therefore, the Ark was kept, that place became the holiest shrine, and the priests of that shrine, if they possessed any power of leadership at all, might be regarded as heads of the people.

At this time the Ark of God was at the city of Shiloh. For that reason Shiloh became the most important city in the land. Israel had no central government and no rulers over the whole nation. The only leaders whom all the people respected were the priests at Shiloh. Every Israelite who could afford it made a pilgrimage to Shiloh at least once a year, and brought gifts and offerings to the sanctuary. Often they asked the advice of God, which the priest gave by consulting the *Urim*[1] and the *Tumim*.[1] They brought sacrifices and they spent the feasts joyously there. When at Shiloh men of Israel felt that they were one people.

IN ANSWER TO OUR PROBLEM

How shall we now answer the questions which we asked at the beginning of this section? Did the conquest help Israel to become a united nation? It seemed at first as though the natural barriers be-

[1] See page 317.

tween regions, the mountains, rivers and plains, would destroy the union which Moses succeeded in cementing. The imitation of Canaanite examples, particularly in worship, further drew the various sections apart from one another. However, the feeling of kinship still remained and asserted itself in time of danger. Above all, the worship of their common God Y, the God of the Wilderness, whose shrine was at Shiloh, served as a reminder. Thus when an outside enemy threatened the land, a strong leader, a chieftain or judge, was able to rally some of the neighboring tribes to act together under the banner of Y. Every united undertaking thus brought the various parts closer together. With Gideon there was already the desire to set up a kingship, that is, a united people under single rule.

Dangers seemed to be quickly forgotten, and the influence of the central sanctuary was only slightly felt while there was peace in the land; but a new enemy was soon to appear, stronger and more dangerous than any which Israel had yet encountered. In the face of this foe the tribes were forced to unite more firmly than ever before, and the struggle lasted so long that the Union which Israel formed for its defense remained permanent. Let us turn to the last chapter in the story of Israel's struggle for union, brought about by the fierce wars with its neighbors of the Coastal Plain, the Philistines.

SUPPLEMENTARY WORK

MAP EXERCISES

1. Israel is already in possession of large parts of Canaan. From section three we recall the physical features of the land and its fertility. Let us now see which sections Israel occupied.

On an outline map let us do the following:

Shade green the territory which the Israelites occupied without any difficulty.

Shade yellow the districts which were finally won after a struggle.

Leave unshaded the parts which the Israelites did not conquer at all.

Fill in the names of all countries, and also Mt. Carmel, The Dead Sea, Chinnereth, and the following cities:

Gaza, Beer Sheba, Hebron, Jerusalem, Jericho, Shechem, Jaffa, Damascus, Tyre.

2. You undoubtedly know that many Jews have settled in Palestine in recent years. Turn to the map of modern Palestine, page 158. The shaded sections represent lands owned by Jews. The names given are of cities which are important today. On an outline map shade the lands which the Jews now own in Palestine. Fill in the names which the various districts bore at the time of the conquests. Include all the names suggested in the third paragraph of the first map exercise following section III which begins "draw dotted line." Near each shaded portion draw a small circle and write within it either

I, meaning that the district was Israelitish or NI, that it was not Israelitish during the period of the conquest.

SUGGESTIONS FOR BIBLE STUDY

There are many chapters in the Bible describing the events of this period, but you might do best to read a selected account in Jacob D. Schwarz—*Into the Promised Land*, pp. 1–34.

QUESTIONS FOR THOUGHT AND DISCUSSION

1. Just as our ancestors tried to form a union among their own tribes, so the nations of the world are trying to join together in some manner today. Do you know anything about the union of nations? Is it already successful? Why do you think it is so hard to form a true union of all nations?
2. Does Palestine suffer from nomadic raids today? Are nomads as dangerous today as they were in ancient times?
3. Were the dangers which threatened the union of Israel helpful or harmful to our ancestors? Are dangers today good or harmful?
4. Who are some famous women in history whom you could compare with Deborah?
5. Do you believe that the first hundred years of life in Canaan spelled progress or backward movement for our ancestors?
6. The ancient Canaanites believed that their Baalim ruled only over one small district. We today believe that all the nations have but one God. What difference should such a belief make in our conduct toward other peoples? Do we truly act as though we believed all nations to be children of one God?

7. Can you think of any differences between the conduct of persons having different gods for various interests such as agriculture, war or poetry, and those having one God over all departments of life?

8. Did the great crisis of the American colonies, namely, the Revolutionary War, unite them at once or did a long time pass before a perfect union was formed? How many years were required before the union became "one and indivisible"? How long a time passed between the first settlement of America and the final union? What would you say then about the difficulty of forming unions in earlier times?

ADDITIONAL READINGS

FOR PUPILS

Hunting, *op. cit.*, pp. 66–73.

Bonser, *op. cit.*, pp. 218–224. This reference is to a play, entitled a "Royal Friendship"; also the story of David, pp. 236.

Wither, George, "The Song of Deborah and Barak." A poem in Kohut, George Alexander, *A Hebrew Anthology*, pp. 130–132. Cincinnati, S. Bacharach, 1913.

Dubnow, S. M., *op. cit.*, Vol. I, pp. 92–120.

(Fiction)—Brady, T. C., *When the Sun Stood Still*. New York, Fleming H. Revell Co., 1917.

A tale of the days of Joshua.

FOR TEACHERS

Noyes, *op. cit.*, pp. 72–136.

Bailey & Kent, *op. cit.*, pp. 59–79.

Kent, *op. cit.*, pp. 124–138.

Bertholet, *op. cit.*, Vol. II, pp. 141–147.

McCurdy, *op. cit.*, pp. 163–189, 224–234.

Margolis & Marx, *op. cit.*, pp. 22–34.

Section V

How Did Israel Become a United Kingdom?

The
PHILISTINES
RIVAL ISRAEL

PHŒNICIANS

ARAMEANS

DAMASCUS

MEDITERRANEAN SEA

DAN

PHILISTINES CANAANITES

Mt. Carmel

Plain of Esdraelon

Sea of CHINNERETH

YARMUK

GILEAD

SHECHEM

SHILOH

JAFFA

EKRON

MIZPAH

JERICHO

AMMON

BETH-SHEMESH
GATH

JERUSALEM

ASHDOD

JUDAH

ASHKELON
DAN
YARMUTH

GAZA

HEBRON

RIVER ARNON

BEERSHEBA

MOAB

EDOM

HEBREWS
PHILISTINES
TRADE ROUTES

MILES
0 5 10 20 30

34°

33°

32°

31°

33°

34°

THE Greatest Danger Was Still to Be Met.

The joined efforts of several tribes had been sufficient to repulse earlier invasions.

But a new foe appeared, the Philistines, *as powerful as Israel itself, and far better equipped for warfare.* In the first encounter Israel suffered a rout. It lost its land to the Philistines.

Then our ancestors were finally roused to their true need. They needed a permanent union under a central government.

But how was it to be achieved? Who would bring together the proud chieftains, jealous of their independence?

Fortunately, a great leader was living at the time, the greatest since Moses. His name was Samuel, and you will read about his labors in this section.

As a result of Samuel's efforts, the Hebrew Kingdom came into being. Saul was the first king.

Saul's Kingdom began very favorably. *It achieved much for Israel, but it did not last long, only about 15 years, from 1028 B.C.E. to 1013 B.C.E.* It seemed to end in defeat and failure.

What did Saul accomplish for his country? Did he benefit his people in any way? *And what opinion*

*should we have of Saul himself, and of his brave
son Jonathan? Let us read our text first and then
think the matter through for ourselves.*

*And finally we come to David, the greatest of Israel's
kings.*

The kingdom became established with David.

The kingdom became an empire and a world power.

What did David do? Why is he considered so much
greater than Saul? *What does Israel owe to
David? That, too, we shall find in the story of
this section.*

*David reigned for forty years after Saul. You should
therefore place David on your time line.*

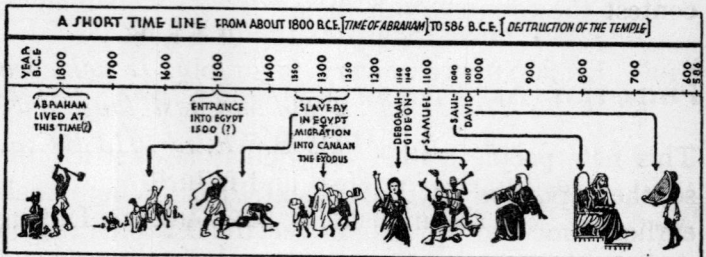

A SHORT TIME LINE — FROM ABOUT 1800 B.C.E. [TIME OF ABRAHAM] TO 586 B.C.E. [DESTRUCTION OF THE TEMPLE]

How Did Israel Become a United Kingdom?

PART I

THE Hebrew tribes had succeeded in occupying Canaan. They had won the Plain of Esdraelon and had penetrated most of the fortified cities. Very few strongholds aside from the city of Jerusalem now remained in Canaanite hands.

Yet the Hebrews were far from secure in their new homes. The eastern and southern frontiers lay open to raids from desert nomads. Disunited as the several groups of tribes were, they could hope to resist an invasion no better than had the small Canaanite kingdoms before them. An immediate danger lay in the west: a nation which had arrived in Canaan as recently as the Hebrews was preparing to contest the country with them.

PHILISTINES ARE RIVALS FOR MASTERY OVER CANAAN

This new people, called the Philistines, settled the southern portion of the Coastal Plain. Where their earlier home had been is not certain. There is reason to believe that they were of Greek origin, having

187

lived in the Island of Crete where they had known
a high degree of civilization. They seem to have been
acquainted with many arts, such as building, forging
iron and bronze, and navigation. They seemed, also,
accustomed to political organization, uniting their
cities in a common federation. An unsuccessful war
drove them from their homes, and they roved the
seas. They were repulsed by the Egyptians, but
finally seized the Eastern Mediterranean shore.
There they established themselves, mainly in five
large cities, which they bound in a common offensive
and defensive union. One of these cities was on the
sea; the other four were inland on the main trade
routes. Their position gave them command over all
caravan trade between Egypt and the northern
countries. Caravans had to pray for protection to all
countries through which they passed. The merchants
also stopped to purchase supplies and to trade with
the cities on the way. Thus, the fact that they were
united, the excellence of their soil and their position
on the main avenues of commerce early made the
Philistines a powerful neighbor and rival for the
mastery of Canaan.

Endanger the Hebrew Settlements

The nearest Hebrew neighbor of the Philistines was
the tribe of Dan, whose territory lay in the Shephela,
the low hills between Judah and Philistia. Dan was

A PHILISTINE AS HE APPEARS ON A MONUMENT

By his face we can tell that he is not of the same race as the Hebrews or Canaanites but is most likely a Greek.

the first tribe to experience the power of the Philistines, and for many years kept up a guerilla warfare against them. The Danite hero of these Philistine encounters is the hero and judge, Samson, whose adventures are related in many thrilling chapters of the Bible. Samson, we are told, was in the habit of visiting the Philistine villages. On one of these visits Samson selected a Philistine girl for his bride. When her parents in his absence married her to another man, Samson sought vengeance in burning the Philistine crops. Thereafter, when the Philistines captured him and thought they had bound him safely, he broke his bonds and slew a thousand of them with the jawbone of an ass, which he found on the ground. Finally, Samson fell into the hands of the Philistines, who blinded him and set him to work at the grindstones in prison. Samson, however, avenged himself upon his enemies. Brought to the Temple of

After Doré

SAMSON THROWS DOWN THE PILLARS

As the artist imagined it.

Dagon to be exhibited in triumph, he pulled down upon the heads of the Philistine worshippers the pillars which supported the roof of their Temple, and perished together with the assembled crowd.[1]

However, these encounters ended disastrously for the tribe of Dan, which was forced to leave its territory and seek a new home. Dan was obliged to migrate to the northernmost point of the Hebrew settlement, where it succeeded in conquering a strip of territory. Thereafter it remained the northern outpost of the Hebrew tribes.

Invade Territory of Northern Israel

Judah, too, seems to have made its peace with the Philistines on terms favorable to its stronger neighbors. But the Philistines probably treated Judah mildly, for Judah, with its steep mountains and narrow passes, was hard to invade.

Northern Israel was not so difficult to penetrate. Strong armies could readily be poured through the vale of Dothan into the broad vale of Esdraelon. From the plain many passes led into the heart of the land of Ephraim. Besides, the land of Ephraim was much more fertile than Judah and, therefore, a more desirable prize.

---

[1] The Samson stories are only partly valuable as history. Their main appeal is as literature. You will enjoy reading them from the Bible or a book of Bible stories. We need not repeat them in full here.

Accordingly the five city kingdoms of the Philistines—Gaza, Ashdod, Ashkelon, Ekron and Gath—organized an invasion against the land of Israel. They marched northward through the Plain of Sharon and encamped at Eben-ezer.

Overrun Israel

The time was most unfortunate for Israel. The only recognized leader was the aged high-priest of Shiloh, named Eli. The military leadership was entrusted to his two sons, Hofni and Phineas, who seem not to have stood high in popular confidence.

It was a gloomy dispirited army which went out to battle, and the results were what might have been expected. In the first encounter Israel was defeated, and the army was forced to retreat with heavy losses.

A hasty council of war, called to plan final heroic measures, decided to bring the Ark of their God into the battle. Y would certainly scatter his enemies. Yet even the Ark failed to bring victory. The battle which followed ended in a rout for Israel. Hofni and Phineas, together with other chiefs, were slain and the Israelites fled from the battlefield. Everything was lost; even the Ark of the Covenant fell into Philistine hands. Israel was now without a country and without a God. Their God had deserted them, or else he was no longer strong. The aged Eli died upon receiving the terrible news. The Philistines took pos-

GAZA—CITY OF THE PHILISTINES

This is the site of Gaza, one of the five main cities of the Philistines. Gaza is the southern outpost between Palestine and the desert, and must have been a very important stopping place for caravans in ancient times. Today it is one of the railroad stations between Palestine and Egypt.

session of the country, stationing their soldiers and military governors in all the walled cities. Israel's freedom was at an end.

The Philistine soldiers guarded carefully against any attempt at revolt. The possession of arms and even the making of arms were forbidden. No Israelite might ply the blacksmith's trade; and, if a farmer wished to mend his plow or sharpen his scythe, he had to go to the smithy in the Philistine village. Worst of all, the Israelites believed that their God, *Y*, had proven powerless against Dagon, god of the Philistines.

Philistines Afraid, Return the Ark

For a moment Israel felt a little encouragement. Israelitish farmers, plowing their fields at Beth-Shemesh near the Philistine border, saw approaching a wagon drawn by young cows. In the wagon stood the Ark of the Lord amidst costly offerings of pure gold, the gifts of the Philistine princes. Later the Israelites learned what had happened in Philistia.

THE ARK

In which were kept the tablets of stone, as the artist imagined it from the biblical description. Notice the cherubim above the ark.

BETH-SHEMESH

Site of the ancient city where the Ark arrived in a driverless wagon
from the land of the Philistines. Beth-Shemesh was on the border
between Judah and Philistia.

The captured Ark had been brought by the tri-
umphant Philistines to their city of Ashdod and
placed alongside of the god Dagon. It happened that
shortly after the Ark was brought into the city a
plague broke out. The superstitious Philistines, be-
lieving the epidemic to be a punishment from the
God of Israel, hurriedly sent the Ark off to the next
city. "Let Gath bear the anger of the God," they
thought. The epidemic spread to Gath. The no less
superstitious citizens of Gath insisted that the Ark
be sent on to Ashkelon. The epidemic, however,
reached Ashkelon, too. No other city would risk in-

viting the vengeance of the God of Israel. It was, therefore, decided to send the God back to his own country to quiet his anger. Thus, it happened that the Ark, borne along in a driverless wagon, found its way among the Israelites.

However, the Ark could no longer inspire the confidence of former days. Since it had failed Israel in war, no city cared to receive it. The Ark was finally placed in the house of a private man where it remained almost forgotten for many years, and Israel continued under the rule of the Philistines.

How Did the Philistine Defeat Affect Israel?

How was Israel to overthrow its conqueror and again become a free people? We shall find that our ancestors were able to rally in spite of their severe losses, because their defeats taught them the valuable lesson that they could be strong only as a united people. Our ancestors were fortunate, too, that at this time there lived a leader, Samuel, who was able to carry the desire for union to fulfilment. Although the formation of the union was still difficult, requiring several efforts before success could be achieved, the work of Samuel and hatred of the Philistines finally made possible a united Hebrew kingdom. Let us see, therefore, how the desire for union found expression, what share Samuel had in its formation, and how successful it proved after it was established.

Defeat Rouses Desire for Union

Israel was unwilling to give up its hard won land as an easy prize to an invader. The braver among the tribes began to speak openly of rebellion. Seers, priests, and especially the "Sons of the Prophets," bands of singing, dancing preachers with flutes and drums, traveled through the land rousing their fellow countrymen to great religious excitement and enthusiasm. These "Sons of the Prophets" were a very important factor in uniting the nation of Israel. However, Israel owes its union mainly to one great seer, to the priest and prophet who alone remained the representative of the God of Shiloh, to Samuel.

The Founder of the Union, Samuel
(About 1100–1020 B.C.E.)

Of all the great leaders who helped Israel through its early troubled period, Samuel stands out as the greatest, as the one who accomplished most for his brethren. Moses began the formation of the Jewish nation, and Samuel completed it: this is what later generations said of Samuel. Samuel has been looked upon as the second deliverer. Like Moses, Samuel worked not for his tribe alone, but for all Israel. Like Moses, he was chiefly the man of God, the religious leader and judge of the people.

Samuel was born of a wealthy Ephraimite family. The Bible tells that his mother, Hannah, who had been childless for many years, used to go to Shiloh every year to pray that God grant her a son. As soon as Samuel was weaned, his pious mother gave him over to the shrine, to be brought up as a holy man and priest, and to be a special servant of God all his life.

Samuel must still have been a young man when the terrible tidings of Eben-ezer reached him. Israel lost its freedom, and Shiloh lost its sanctuary; Samuel remained a priest without his God and without his temple.

ASSUMES LEADERSHIP AT FALL OF SHILOH

With the passing of time the wounds of the defeat began to heal. Common suffering brought the separated tribes more closely together. Perhaps, they thought, they had disobeyed their God or had angered him by the worship of the *Baalim*. If only there were a Shiloh again, where they might all come together. Shiloh was no more, but one of the holy men of Shiloh still remained. This holy man did not wait for the people to come to seek him. He went among them, from city to city, and taught them. Soon men came to ask the word of God from him as they had gone to Eli before. They came to him to consult the oracle, or to have him adjudge their quarrels, regarding him as the high priest and the sanctuary in one.

Generally, when we think of the early seers, we have in mind persons who were much like fortune tellers. The seers were regarded as magic priests who could give advice by casting the sacred lots. They were consulted about articles that had been lost, the success of journeys that were being planned, about raids and other ventures.

SEER AND STATESMAN

Samuel, while still somewhat a seer, stands out already as a prophet. He was like the seers of his day in that men still came to him to seek the sacred lots and asked the usual advice. We shall soon see, for example, how Saul came to ask Samuel about some donkeys which went astray. Yet Samuel was far more than a seer: he was an outstanding leader of his people. Two elements distinguished Samuel from other seers. Samuel was mainly occupied with his people's problems rather than with his lots. He was constantly traveling from city to city, adjusting disputes, and keeping alive the memory of the wilderness days and of their common God. In time everyone accepted him as Israel's uncrowned leader. It was no small achievement to win the confidence of the many rival tribal chiefs. Many weary journeys, much earnest pleading and, above all, a commanding personality must have been required to awaken hopes in defeated Israel and to get the tribes to agree upon common action.

TEACHER

Equally important to Samuel, the statesman, was Samuel, the religious teacher. Other seers were concerned merely with what was lucky or unlucky, with the telling of fortunes. Samuel was a moral teacher, a teacher of righteousness. Continuing the religion of Moses, he reminded his fellow Israelites that their God Y was mainly concerned with human conduct. He may even have pointed out that their present plight was the result of their having angered their God by wrongful acts. Y demanded not sacrifice, but obedience. Samuel's own life must have been an example of his teaching, for in his old age, relates the Bible, the prophet invited criticism of his acts and asked anyone who had any claims against him to present them.[1]

Stirs Desire for Union

At festivals the chiefs of the various tribes gathered at Ramah, Samuel's home, for sacrifice and festivity. As these leaders of the tribes sat about the banquet board, it was natural that they should discuss the

[1] I Samuel chap. XII, v. 3

AN ARAB FEAST

To this day the Arab meals are served out of doors as in the days
of Abraham. Notice that their table manners are somewhat different from ours. They seem to have no use for knives and forks,
but use their fingers. The food is sometimes quite hot.

affairs of the land. What more important question
could come before them than that of the hated
Philistines? The elders of the tribes were beginning
to recognize the cause of Israel's weakness in the
tribal strife and jealousy which were destroying the
strength of the nation. They must now form one
government over the tribes after the manner of the
Philistines who chose the bravest and most warlike
chieftain their king.

The hands of time had turned; and now, after several hundred years, the heads of the tribes were ready

to do what before only the power of Moses' leadership could force upon them. After these many years
had passed, they were again ready to form one
Israelitish family with the God of Israel at its head.
Who at such a time was more fitted to organize this
family and to choose its king than the chief priest of
God? To Samuel, therefore, they came with the request that he choose a king for them.

Samuel Seeks a Candidate

Who was to be the king to unite them? Samuel may
have wished that a priest-king head the people so
that Y might truly be their king; but the prophet
understood that the danger which threatened called
for a warrior-king.

The story of the choice of the first king is not entirely clear. According to the biblical tale, Saul, the
son of Kish, a member of one of the leading families
of the tribe of Benjamin, was seeking his father's
lost donkeys. Passing by the city of Zuph and
hearing that Samuel was there to celebrate a feast,
he stopped to inquire of the seer about the where-
abouts of the donkeys. Saul's powerful figure and
courtly bearing must have impressed Samuel, for he
felt that he now had a likely candidate for the kingship. It may be that Samuel confided his thoughts to
Saul, though the latter returned to his plowing as
though nothing unusual had occurred.

JABESH-GILEAD

Site of the ancient city in East Jordan where Saul first proved himself deserving of the crown of Israel. The ruins which you see are of temples and palaces built by Romans many centuries later.

Saul Proves Himself at Jabesh-Gilead

Soon an occasion presented itself which showed Samuel that his choice had been wise. While Canaan, west of the Jordan, was overrun by the Philistines, the King of Ammon thought it a good opportunity to invade the Israelite territory east of the Jordan, the land of Gilead. He laid siege to one of the principal towns, Jabesh-Gilead, and demanded that the inhabitants surrender. The King of Ammon, however, was not satisfied with mere submission. According to the custom of the time, a king displayed his heroism by disfiguring his prisoners. The King of Ammon, desiring to make his victory particularly impressive to his subjects, demanded as a condition of surrender that each male in the garrison have his right eye gouged out.

The starved and war-weary city could do nothing but yield even upon these inhuman conditions; yet it decided to try one last means of saving itself. It would hold out for a short while, till it could send for aid to its brethren west of the Jordan. Further resistance, it is true, might cost the citizens of the city not only their sight, but their lives; but they decided to run the risk. Messengers came to Ephraim and to Benjamin; and, among other places, they visited Geba, the home of Saul.

The people were deeply moved by the sad fate which awaited Jabesh-Gilead; but there was no one who could offer any suggestion of help. Saul was then returning from his field with his oxen and his plow. Inquiring about the cause of the commotion, he was told of the mission from Gilead. Straightway Saul cut up into pieces the oxen with which he was plowing and, giving them to the messengers, instructed them to go among the tribes and proclaim, "Whosoever

THE ANOINTING OF SAUL
As the artist imagined it.

After Doré

cometh not forth after Saul and after Samuel, so shall it be done unto his oxen." [1]

The call to arms aroused great enthusiasm among the Israelites. The labor of Samuel and their common danger had brought them much closer together than in former days. Before night an army was assembled, crossed the Jordan and surprised the Ammonites. Jabesh-Gilead was saved through the heroism of Saul. Saul had proved himself the worthy leader of a united Israel.

Saul Crowned King of Israel—1028 B.C.E.

Samuel now assembled the elders of all the tribes and publicly proclaimed Saul the first king over all Israel. Even Judah was included in this federation. The first kingly government was organized. Saul made the beginnings of a regular army through the selection of a bodyguard of the bravest warriors, in whose charge he placed the enforcement of his laws. When a war was to be fought, however, Saul could call upon all fighting men to take up arms. The government set up by Saul was still very simple, consisting of few officers. There was as yet no capital, nor any kingly palace. We cannot say much more about this early kingdom, because we really know very little about Saul's reign except what the Bible tells us, and in the Bible only a very brief account is given.

[1] I Samuel, chap. II, v. 7

How Successful Was the First Hebrew King?

After almost two centuries of occupation of Canaan, the Hebrew tribes were at last united under the rule of a single king. How successful was this first kingdom to prove? Would it be able to retain the loyalty of the separate tribes which had at all times considered themselves independent? Above all, would it be able to regain the land from the Philistines? Let us see how far the kingdom of Saul was successful and wherein it proved weak.

The Successes of Saul's Kingdom

Saul had been chosen king for a special reason. The Israelites were eager to throw off the yoke of the Philistines. They, therefore, chose a king who would lead them against the hated conquerors. Now that Israel had been tested in battle against Ammon, Saul thought it a proper time to undertake an attack against the Philistine garrisons which were stationed in the heart of the country.

Victory over Philistines

The signal for an uprising was an attack by Jonathan, son of Saul, upon the Philistine governor at Geba, his home city. The governor, taken altogether

MICHMASH

Where Jonathan and his armor-bearer climbed through the narrow
gorge and fell single-handed upon the Philistines.

unawares, was forced to retreat, and this first victory encouraged many Israelites to join Saul's
army. However, when the Philistines, soon thereafter, gathered a large army and prepared to punish
Saul for the rebellion, the greater part of Saul's
army deserted him.

The victory over the Philistines was won by Jonathan, who went against the Philistines single-handed,
with only his armor-bearer to help him. A strong out-

post of Philistines had been encamped at the foot of the mountains in a ravine that could be reached only by a narrow path, on either side of which were steep rocks. Jonathan, followed by his attendant, secretly climbed up the pass and then charged upon the Philistines.

The enemy, unable to imagine that only two men would dare to come within their camp, thought that the whole Israelite army was upon them. They were thrown into confusion, and their disorder was soon discovered by the Israelite army. Saul now hastened to attack the Philistines with the 600 men who remained with him. Many Israelites also left their places of hiding to join in the pursuit. The Israelite victory was complete, and the land was freed from the Philistines for the time.

Victorious against Amelek

Saul followed up his victory over the Philistines by subduing another enemy of his kingdom. The Amalekites, whose territory lay somewhere south of Judah carried on a feud with Israel that may have dated back from the days of Kadesh-Barnea. A battle with Amalek is reported as having taken place during the life of Moses.

Saul now proceeded against these tribesmen, defeated them decisively, and returned with much valuable material.

Saul's Authority Recognized

Saul's successes established his authority throughout the tribes of Israel, and there is no record of any rebellion during his reign. From Dan in the north to Judah in the south, Saul's rule was recognized and feared. Saul's government was still new and inexperienced. His land was not as peaceable as are most countries of today. Outlaws, nomadic spirits who could not accustom themselves to settled life, or unsuccessful farmers who were unable to pay their debts made many mountain districts unsafe for travel. Most of the tasks of government still remained with the village elders. The king's court looked little more than the residence of an important chieftain. Yet the king kept the land secure against foreign enemies and, above all, through him Israel was united. Israel could well be proud of its king, whose fearless courage had brought it peace and honor. The king's brave sons, too, and the king's cousin, Abner, his general-in-chief, formed a company of heroes about whose bravery many tales are told.

Fortune Turns against Saul

New difficulties were now arising for Saul, weakening his kingdom and endangering the unity of Israel. Three causes worked against the king. The first of

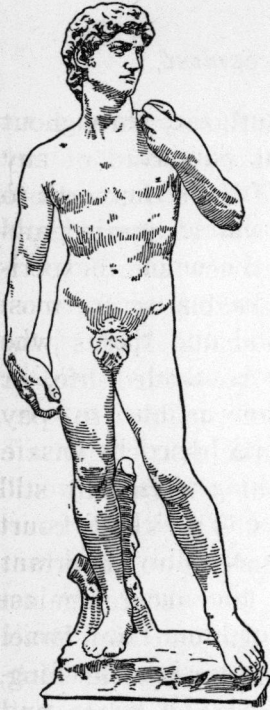

DAVID

As the artist imagined him.

these arose from a quarrel with Samuel, which deprived Saul of the advice of the most highly revered man of God. The second is to be found in a mental illness, a melancholia, a fear and a sadness which crept upon Saul. When this fear seized him, Saul would become angry and unapproachable even to his family and his captains. At such times the government would suffer, for the king was not in a condition to look after it.

The third cause may be traced to the arrival at Saul's court of a young man from Judah, David by name, who achieved such great glory that the king saw in him a rival for the throne. A long strife followed between Saul and David. The latter sought safety among his own tribesmen, the Judeans. While these feared to help David openly against Saul, their sympathy for David must have greatly weakened the bond of union between Israel and Judah. We shall see now how each of these three causes wrought harm to Saul's kingdom.

Saul's Quarrel with Samuel

The Bible tells very little about the reasons for Samuel's disagreement with Saul. Samuel, the great leader of his people, who knew of the struggle which Israel had undergone to become united, would probably be careful not to endanger the union; but it is natural that disagreement should have arisen between the authority of the man of God and that of the king. It may be that Saul, who was mainly a soldier, did not understand and did not show as much interest in the religion of Y as Samuel had hoped he would. Perhaps Samuel dreamed that a king of Israel would set up the Ark again at some place to which all Israel might come at the holy seasons. Possibly Saul was not entirely ready to introduce the many new reforms which Samuel demanded of him. Thus, while Saul supposedly ordered the suppression of witchcraft, he himself did not truly give up his belief in it. The aged prophet, therefore, withdrew from public life to continue quietly his work as the great religious teacher and seer of his time.

The disagreement with the holy man must have estranged many from the king. It must also have made Saul feel that God was not with him any more. For a moody man like Saul this was a serious matter, and he now began to suffer from more frequent fits of terror than formerly.

THE KINGDOM OF SAUL

MEDITERRANEAN SEA

PHŒNICIANS

ARAMEANS

DAMASCUS

CANAANITES

Mt. Carmel

Sea of CHINNERETH

DAN

River Jordan

GILEAD

JABESH-GILEAD

GILBOA

SHECHEM

SHILOH

EKRON

MIZPAH

GEBA

NOB

JERICHO

ASHDOD

JERUSALEM

GATH

YARMUTH

ASHKELON

HEBRON

GAZA

JUDAH

ZIKLAG

BEER-SHEBA

RIVER ARNON

AMMON

MOAB

AMALEKITES

EDOM

TRADE ROUTES

MILES

Saul's Melancholy—Quarrel with David

After the quarrel with Samuel, Saul frequently suffered from attacks of melancholy. His officers, finding that music eased the distressed king, advised that he invite to his court a Judean shepherd lad who was known to play beautifully upon the harp. This was the introduction to the king's court of the famous David, who was to be the final successful upbuilder of a united Israel and who was to be the ideal king of Israel, the symbol of its strength and unity.

David rapidly rose in fame in the king's household. Not only did he play the harp as no one else in Israel, but he was found to be an even greater warrior and, above all, an able leader. In the constant warfare with which Saul's reign was filled, David had ample opportunity to display his valor. David became the most dreaded name among the Philistines, and the most talked of in Israel. Although the young hero was descended from a humble Judean family, the king was ready to give him his own daughter in marriage. Jonathan, the son of Saul, famed for his bravery and best beloved among the people, was David's closest friend.

Surely Saul should have been happy. In David he had found a worthy addition to Abner and his son Jonathan; but, when his melancholy mood attacked Saul, terror would seize him and he would fear that his own household was turning against him. Particularly was his fear aroused by the great popularity of his new general. Whenever David returned from the war, the maidens used to meet him in procession, singing and dancing before him. What angered the king especially was a new song which the maidens were singing: "Saul hath slain his thousands, and David his ten thousands."[1] Was not Saul chosen because he was the bravest and strongest of the chiefs, and would not the people depose him if they found a more capable leader?

DAVID FORCED TO FLEE COURT

The great love and confidence which the king bore David were now turning to fear and hate. Although the king had promised David his daughter, he now demanded that David bring one hundred trophies from slain Philistines before he would consent to the marriage. David brought the king what he asked for, and did finally marry Saul's daughter, Michal; but the jealousy of the king increased, and David was obliged to flee the court and find hiding in the mountains and caves of his native Judah.

Saul's anger increased when he learned of David's escape. It was reported to him that on his way to Judah, David had visited the sanctuary at Nob, where the priests who were descendants of the house

[1] I Samuel, chap. VIII, v. 7

of Eli had established themselves. David had in the past frequently stopped there on his way to battle to consult the oracle. The unsuspecting priests advised David as usual, and even gave him provisions. When the king heard of this, he accused the priests of treason and ordered them to be executed. Only one priest, Abiathar, succeeded in escaping to Judah where he joined the fugitive David. The slaughter of the priests was intended as a terrible example of what the angry king would do to others who might be tempted to give David aid.

In the meantime, David had gathered about him a band of outlaws and lived as a freebooter in the mountains of Judah. This band, consisting of four hundred men, roamed through the Negeb, attacking Edomites, Amalekites and other nomadic tribes of the region and living upon the captured booty. David, with the aid of his men, also guarded his fellow Judeans against raids, and in return his countrymen rewarded him with provisions. When the Philistines attacked one of the Judean cities, David's little army could always be called to the rescue.

SAUL PURSUES DAVID

When Saul learned of David's activities, he set out with an army to pursue him. Then it was no longer safe for the Judeans to assist David, for they all remembered the fate of the priests of Nob. The pur-

DAVID'S BAND OF OUTLAWS

After Doré

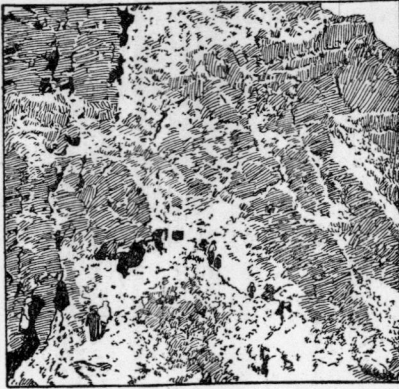

CLIFFS OF EN-GEDI

In the mountains of Judah where Saul pursued David. These cliffs are full of large caves where companies of men can hide.

suit lasted a long time and it was filled with many thrills and adventures. The Bible relates that on several occasions David had Saul in his power, but refused to do injury to Israel's monarch. However, David was being driven further and further into the desert, among tribes with whom he was engaged in blood feuds and at whose hands he might meet his death.

DAVID GOES OVER TO PHILISTINES

In this difficult position David decided upon a desperate measure. When he could no longer find safety among his own people, he would seek it among his people's most dangerous foes. David, the conqueror of the Philistines, decided to offer his services to the Philistine king, Achish of Gath. Achish was most happy to have the arch enemy of the Philistines as his ally. David was given the city of Ziklag for his

men who now numbered six hundred, and in return
he was to render military assistance to his Philistine
master and to bring him booty from Judean villages.

This was a most trying time for David. To bring
the booty he raided not the Judeans, but the tribes
about Judea, the enemies of his own tribe. Yet he
knew that, if Achish learned of what he was doing,
his life would be in danger. It was under such conditions that David lived among the Philistines for more
than a year.

First Kingdom Ends Disastrously

There had been war between the Philistines and the
Israelites during all the days of Saul. While David
had fought for Israel, matters went badly for the
Philistines. Now, however, as an ally of the Philistines, he was pledged to fight against his own people.
Saul's fears and melancholy moods, too, did much to
weaken the confidence of the people in him. The
Philistines naturally thought the time opportune to
regain what they had lost in the land of Israel. A
large host was collected, larger than any which had
yet invaded Israel.

As a follower of Achish, David was obliged to join
him in this war. With a heavy heart David and his
men followed the Philistine armies against their own
brothers, uncertain of what part they would play in
the battle. David still treasured his love for Jona-

than, and his reverence for Israel's fearless monarch
had not diminished. Fortunately for David, the
Philistines themselves helped him out of his difficulties. The Philistine generals were afraid to have an
Israelite in their midst in such a decisive battle. They
looked with suspicion upon the allegiance of David,
their famous enemy who was now fighting in their
ranks, and insisted that Achish send David back to
Ziklag. David returned to his home in time to pursue
some raiders who had attacked Ziklag in his absence.

SAUL'S LAST BATTLE

Saul heard of the preparations by the Philistines and
hastened to gather his forces. It was no new thing
for Saul to battle with the Philistines, yet he was
feeling oppressed and uncertain about the outcome.
The Philistines had massed their troops in the plain
of Jezreel. Saul consulted the oracle, but the answer
was unfavorable. Then, we are told, in despair Saul
sought out a witch who, he believed, would bring up
the dead Samuel to advise him. The results of this
visit were even more disheartening than the oracle
had been. Saul's brooding overwhelmed him. He knew
that the battle was lost; but, brave to the end, he
would do his duty even if he had to die fighting.

The battle was fought at the foot of Mt. Gilboa.
The Israelites suffered a decisive rout, as disastrous
as in the battle with the Philistines in the days of

Eli. Saul, falling wounded, took his life with his own sword. Jonathan, too, gave his life for his people. So now the Philistines again became masters of the land. There was no one to oppose them. The remains of Saul's army under Abner fled to East Jordan. Saul's kingship over a united Israel had come to an unhappy end.

David's Lament over Saul

The feelings of the people over their fallen hero were beautifully expressed by the man who had suffered most at his hands. David, who had been driven from his native land by the king's unjust anger, knew, nevertheless, the true qualities of Israel's fallen leader and his sons. David, the patriot and Israel's sweet singer, composed the following lines which are to this day among the most beautiful gems of the Bible.

"And David lamented with this lamentation over Saul and over Jonathan his son:

"Thy beauty, O Israel, upon thy high places is slain!
How are the mighty fallen!
Tell it not in Gath,
Publish it not in the streets of Ashkelon;
Lest the daughters of the Philistines rejoice,
Lest the daughters of the uncircumcised triumph.
Ye mountains of Gilboa,

Let there be no dew nor rain upon you,
Neither fields of choice fruits;
For there the shield of the mighty was vilely cast
     away,
The shield of Saul, not anointed with oil.
From the blood of the slain, from the fat of the
     mighty,
The bow of Jonathan turned not back,
And the sword of Saul returned not empty.

Saul and Jonathan, the lovely and the pleasant
In their lives, even in their death they were not
     divided;
They were swifter than eagles,
They were stronger than lions.
Ye daughters of Israel, weep over Saul,
Who clothed you in scarlet, with other delights,
Who put ornaments of gold upon your apparel.
How are the mighty fallen in the midst of the
     battle!

Jonathan upon thy high places is slain!
I am distressed for thee, my brother Jonathan;
Very pleasant hast thou been unto me;
Wonderful was thy love to me,
Passing the love of women.
How are the mighty fallen,
And the weapons of war perished!" [1]

[1] II Samuel, chap. I, 17, 19–27

The Gratitude of Jabesh-Gilead

The men of Jabesh-Gilead, too, expressed their devotion to the fallen heroes who had at one time been their saviors. During the night they stole into the camp of the Philistines and rescued the bodies of Saul and his sons which the Philistines were displaying in triumph. Saul found his final resting place in the city of his first triumph, at Jabesh-Gilead.

PART II

SUCCESSFUL UNION ACHIEVED—DAVID
(1013–973 B.C.E.)

We have followed the efforts of our early ancestors to unite into one nation. Years of struggle against foreign oppressors and many disastrous wars seemed to have brought the lesson home. At last, when Israel had already learned the value of union and was prepared to live under one king, the crushing defeat at the hands of the Philistines seemed to end their hopes of becoming a large unified people. A mere shadow of the kingdom was left in East Jordan.

We shall see, however, that the efforts of the two hundred years were not in vain. The realization that it was good to have a king was already well rooted. A king was to come forth who would drive out the

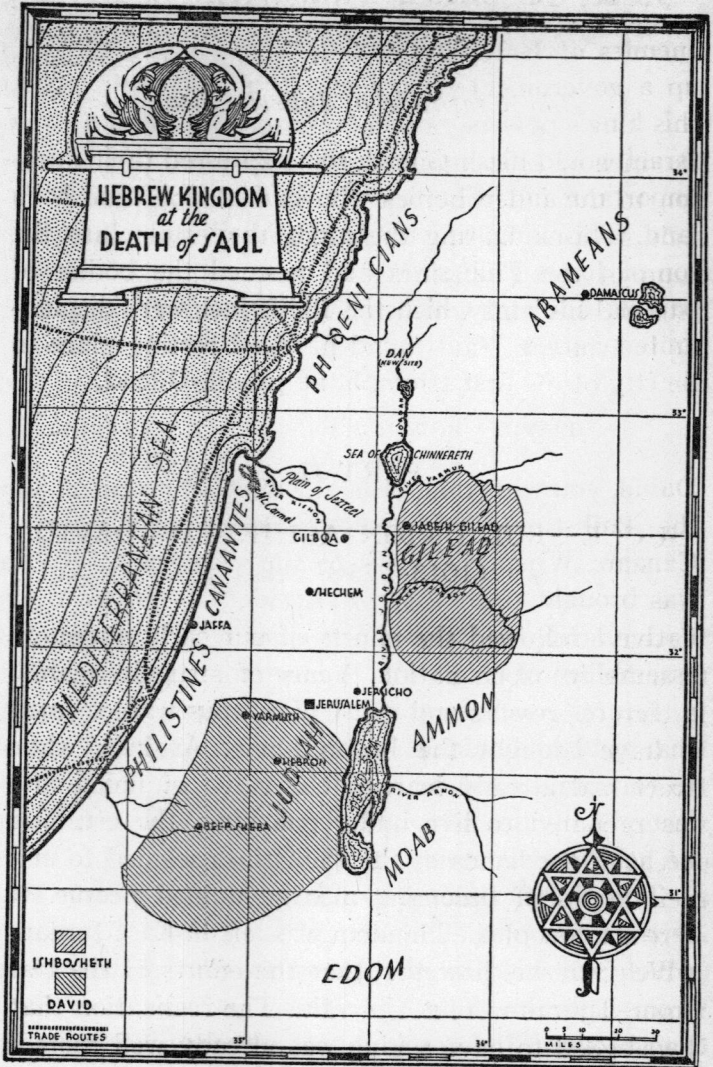

HEBREW KINGDOM
at the
DEATH of SAUL

MEDITERRANEAN SEA

PHOENICIANS

ARAMEANS

● DAMASCUS

DAN
(NEW SITE)

SEA OF CHINNERETH

Plain of Jezreel

Mt. Carmel

PHILISTINES

CANAANITES

JABESH-GILEAD ●

GILEAD

GILBOA ●

● SHECHEM

● JAFFA

● JERICHO

■ JERUSALEM

AMMON

● YARMUTH

JUDAH

● HEBRON

RIVER ARNON

● BEER-SHEBA

MOAB

EDOM

ISHBOSHETH

DAVID

TRADE ROUTES

MILES

enemies of Israel successfully and who would build up a government that would last. With the aid of this king's powers, both as warrior and as statesman, Israel would become not only a nation, but the most important and the most feared nation in the Westland. This king, as you may guess, was David, the son of Jesse. The period of David will close the first part of our story, which tells how Israel became a united nation.

David Crowned King of Judah

David, you will recall, was at Ziklag while Israel and the Philistines were contesting the possession of Canaan. When the news of the disaster at Gilboa was brought to him, David decided to return to his native land. At Hebron, the chief city in Judah, an assemblage of chiefs was to meet to determine about a future government. The Philistines were eager that Judah should choose its own king, in order to encourage civil strife among their conquered subjects. A divided Israel, the Philistines believed, could be held more securely.

The North and the South had always been two separate peoples. The strip of land about Jerusalem which was held by the Jebusites kept Judah apart from Ephraim. The early fame and power of Saul had brought Judah and Israel together, but even in the days of Saul the union was very weak. We have seen how for a long time the South was willing to shelter David, then a rebel against the king. Now that Saul had died, Judah preferred to choose its own king. The choice readily fell upon the most famous war chief, David, who was crowned king of Judah at Hebron.

SEEKS CROWN OF REMAINDER OF TRIBES

Abner, Saul's commander-in-chief, had escaped from Gilboa and assumed the charge of restoring Saul's government. One of Saul's sons, Ish-Bosheth, a weakling in every way and altogether unfitted for the kingship, was still alive. However, since he was the son of the heroic Saul, the Israelites, particularly Saul's tribesmen, the Benjaminites and the Gileadites, crowned him as their king. The capital of Ish-Bosheth was in Mahanaim, east of the Jordan, probably beyond the reach of the Philistines.

DAVID VICTORIOUS

David could foresee little hope of freedom from Philistia with Israel divided into two kingdoms. He felt that at all costs he must unite the tribes, even if it required the use of force. First David tried to win over to his banner the men of Jabesh-Gilead, Saul's strongest supporters. Peace offers failing, war broke out between the North and the South, and David's army was gaining the upper hand. Abner, the main support of Ish-Bosheth, died in a blood feud. Ish-Bosheth himself was treacherously slain by his own captains. The northern tribes, realizing that there was no other leader who could inspire confidence in the entire people, sent their elders as an embassy to David, offering him the crown of Israel. David thus became the second king of all the Hebrew tribes.

David Builder of Hebrew Nation

So long as civil war was going on in Israel, the Philistines remained undisturbed. They were well pleased that David, whom they still considered their ally, was victorious. However, when they heard that David was crowned king over all Israel, they understood that there could be only one purpose in Israel's new union. Rapidly they sent an army to Judah to punish their former ally for having become king without their permission. Thus began the new wars with the Philistines.

Frees Land of Philistines

David's greatest achievement was his victory over the Philistines. He had had long experience in fighting against the Philistines in the days of Saul. In the mountains he was particularly familiar with all the passes and hiding places. David brought the enemy

into positions where their chariots and their cavalry
were useless against the shepherd slingers of Judah.
The wars lasted a long time, although the Bible tells
us but little about them, and only here and there is
mention made of the daring deeds of David's heroes.
Finally, not only were the Philistines driven out of
the Hebrew lands, but the war was successfully carried by David into their own country. The enemy
which had threatened the life of Israel for almost
seventy-five years was at last subdued. David, who
had been crowned king without a land, now laid the
beginnings of a new empire.

Captures Jerusalem

Successful against the Philistines, David undertook
to strengthen the kingdom from within. His first
difficulty was the choice of a capital which would be
the national center for Israel. It must be a city which
would satisfy both the North and the South. Hebron
would not do, because it was the capital of Judah;
moreover, it was too far south. Geba, Saul's capital,
was too prominently in the north, and its location
was not suited for defense. One city exactly met all
of David's requirements: Jerusalem, the city of the
Jebusites, which belonged neither to Ephraim nor to
Judah, but was situated between both and would,
therefore, be truly neutral ground. The city was the
meeting point of all the important trade routes pass-

ing through that part of the country. In addition, nature had so strongly fortified Jerusalem as to make it the mightiest stronghold in all Canaan. Located on the highest part of the Judean mountains, steep cliffs on three sides rendered it practically inaccessible, the only approach to the city being by a path from the north. During all the wars of the conquest the city had remained in the hands of its original Canaanite inhabitants, the Jebusites, and not even Saul could capture it for Israel.

The siege of Jerusalem was another of the great military accomplishments of David. The Jebusites, overconfident of the strength of the city, boasted that their crippled and their lame could protect it against the Israelites. The city did not, however, hold out against David's veterans. It had an underground tunnel leading outside the walls to a spring. David's men discovered the tunnel and through it found their way into the city. Jerusalem thus fell into the hands of the Israelites, who were to make its name famous in the history of the world.

Transfers Capital to New City

David now transferred his government to the new capital. The city consisted of several hills. The hill on which David's palace was located became known as Zion, or the City of David. Mount Zion has since given the name to the entire land, so that the move-

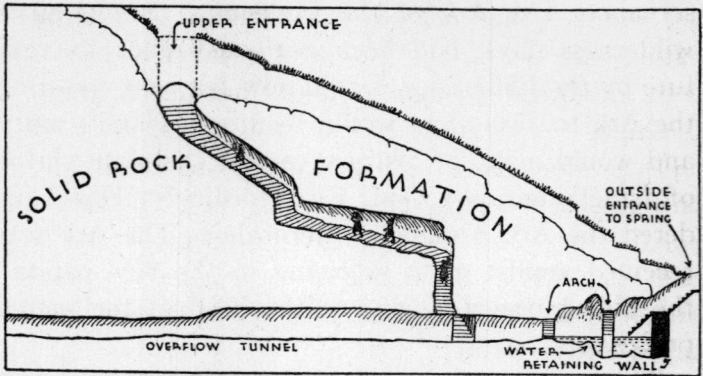

UNDERGROUND TUNNEL AT JERUSALEM

This picture shows a diagram of a secret tunnel which led from the
hill of Zion to a spring outside of the city. The tunnel was reached
at two points by a long flight of steps. From this secret spring
the city was assured of water in time of a siege.

ment for the rebuilding of Palestine is known as
Zionism.

The capture of Jerusalem was the last link to as-
sure Israel's possession of Canaan. The land now was
no longer Canaan; it became "Eretz Yisroel," Land
of Israel, from Dan to the limits of Negeb and from
the plain of the Philistines to the Eastern Desert.
Moses' dream of a united Israel in peaceful possession of its own land, was at last fulfilled.

Brings Ark to Jerusalem—Makes City Main Shrine

David was anxious to make Jerusalem the center
not only of government, but also of religious ob-

servance. The Ark of the Covenant, famous since wilderness days, had been neglected since its capture by the Philistines. David now felt that restoring the Ark to Jerusalem would reenforce Israel's unity and would make of his new capital the main shrine of Israel's national God, *Y*. Accordingly, David ordered the Ark brought to Jerusalem. The Ark was received amidst great rejoicing in the new capital, the king himself dancing at the head of the sacred procession.

The bringing of the Ark to Jerusalem was the first step in making that city the most famous shrine in the world. Hereafter, every Israelite would feel it his duty to visit Jerusalem at each festival. The heathen, too, would be attracted by their curiosity to see how God might be worshipped without idols or images. Shortly a temple was to be built which would play an important part in the life of the people. Thus the foundation for the future greatness of this city was laid by David, and another strong link was forged in the union of Israel.

Secures Valuable Allies

David's fame won for him many allies from among the powerful neighboring kings. When David desired to build a palace for himself, Hiram, king of Tyre, sent skilled workmen from his city, as well as cedarwood. David wanted to build a temple for the Ark,

CEDARS OF LEBANON

These giant trees growing in the Lebanon mountains in Phoenicia were greatly desired for building purposes. King David imported some of these timbers for the building of his palace.

which until then had been housed in a tent. The tent made an appearance of poverty alongside of the new royal palace. The prophet, Nathan, however, advised David against the undertaking. A temple of God, he told David, must be built by a man of peace, not by one who had spent all his years in bloodshed.

Extends Boundaries through Conquests

After David had won back for Israel all the land of its original settlement, he set out to make further conquests in the surrounding countries. Moab and Ammon fell before David's armies. The seaports of Edom, as well as the overland routes from Arabia to Egypt, fell into his hands. The king of Damascus, who tried to help Ammon, was himself defeated and his country added to Israel. David placed gov-

ernors and garrisons in the conquered provinces to
collect tribute which was sent to Jerusalem and
distributed among the fighting men. Israel had become more than a nation; it was now an empire.

Organizes a Government

Saul had tried to rule the country alone. We do not
hear of any officers in Saul's government, or of his
putting any tax upon the nation. David's empire was
too large for him to manage alone; and, being an
organizer as well as a soldier, David laid the foundation for a lasting government. In order to tax the

SIDON

One of the ancient famous trading cities of the Phoenicians. From
this port, trading galleys left to lands as distant as Spain. Sidon
today is a garden village.

people justly and to determine the numbers of fighting men, David wanted to know the number of the population. Accordingly, for the first time since the conquest of Canaan, a census was attempted of Israel and Judah. David also kept a large standing army under able generals. Thus David not only won victories, but also made it possible for Israel to remain united and to reap the fruits of his conquests.

REBELLIONS AGAINST DAVID

Israel had many reasons to be grateful to David. He had recovered the country from the Philistines and even made Israel supreme over Philistia. Israel became the strongest power in the Westland, all the kings of the neighboring countries being either David's vassals or his allies. Yet the roots of disunion were so deep that the various tribes did not yet feel as one. Their loyalty was not centered on the whole people, on their land or their king. Israel and Judah were still two peoples, and any slight disturbance might break the union and again bring disorder in Israel.

Perhaps the nation was weary of the constant wars in which thousands of Israel's young men had fallen, or it may be that the tribal chiefs jealously saw many of their ancient liberties usurped by a king. A spirit of discontent was felt, which a popular leader might use to start a revolution. Men of such ambition were not slow to appear. Two rebellions broke out in close succession. The first was led by the king's own son, Absalom; the second by a Benjamite chieftain, Sheba ben Bichri.

Revolt of Absalom

Absalom, whose beautiful appearance and winning manners made him beloved of the people, thought he could seize the throne by promising reform in the administration of justice. The people were complaining that the king, whose duty it was to act as the

MAHANAIM

In East Jordan where David found refuge when he fled from his son Absalom.

TOMB OF ABSALOM

This monument is located outside of Jerusalem. Most likely it is really the tomb of a king who lived more than eight hundred years later.

supreme judge, was forever too busy with his wars to listen to their grievances. Absalom always kept himself in readiness to listen to all complaints and in a kindly way tried to make peace between both sides. Thus many were led to wish that Absalom really might be king, and the number of Absalom's followers increased so that the ambitious prince was ready to declare his rebellion publicly. Amidst the acclaim of a great multitude, Absalom was crowned king over Judah and Israel in place of his father. David, already an old man, barely escaped with his household to a place of hiding east of the Jordan.

Absalom knew that his throne was unsafe so long as his father was still alive. With a large army he set out to pursue his father. David, however, soon received the support of his veteran generals and his army, who joined him in his retreat. Civil war followed, and David's experienced army was victorious. Absalom's following was scattered, the usurper himself lost his life, and David returned in triumph to Jerusalem.

Rebellion in the North

Hardly had the revolt of Absalom been suppressed, when a Benjamite sheik, Sheba ben Bichri, started a new rebellion of the northern tribes against David. The northern tribes seceded from the Hebrew kingdom and chose Sheba as their ruler. David's well trained army again was at hand to suppress the uprising. Sheba was driven to the northernmost corner of Israel, in the land of Dan, where he was killed by his own followers.

DAVID'S LAST DAYS

David's last days were spent in peace. The king was in ill health; but no further disturbances threatened his kingdom. His subjects were learning to appreciate David's devotion to his people and the great deeds which he had accomplished. As he grew older, his fame increased; and after he died, he became to the people their ideal king and their greatest hero.

DAVID'S TOMB AT JERUSALEM

For many years people have believed this tomb to be that of Israel's great king. Whether David really was buried here is not known.

The tribe of Judah was particularly grateful. David had raised his tribe from the position of lowly shepherds on rocky mountain slopes to that of rulers over proud Ephraim. In the minds of the Judeans, the kingship remained forever connected with the family of David, and no king ever ruled over Jerusalem who could not trace his relationship to the great king. Even after it was exiled from its home, Israel hoped that it would return and reestablish its state under a descendant of the house of David.

SUMMING UP

This is the story of how Israel became a nation. Taught the benefits of union by Moses in their desert wanderings, the Hebrew tribes soon forgot their

EMPIRE *of* DAVID *and* SOLOMON

MEDITERRANEAN SEA

PHOENICIANS

ARAMEANS

SIDON

TYRE

BAN

DAMASCUS

SEA OF CHINNERETH

JABESH-GILEAD

GILEAD

SHECHEM

JAFFA

JERICHO

AMMON

YARMUTH

JERUSALEM

JUDAH

PHIL'S TINES CANAANITES

RIVER ARNON

BEERSHEBA

MOAB

EDOM

ELATH
70 MILES
DUE SOUTH
OF HERE

ARABIA TO THE SOUTH

TRADE ROUTES

MILES

lesson in the early struggles to retain their conquests.
National interests yielded to local needs, and the
worship of their common God became only second
in importance to the worship of the many gods of
Canaan.

The divided country thus became an easy prey for
invasion. As the Israelites had once fallen upon the
land, so other tribes now, in turn, attacked them.
Moreover, the Israelites had not yet completely destroyed the power of the former master of the land,
the Canaanites.

There followed a number of misfortunes, any of
which might have destroyed Israel—the last great
stand of the Canaanite kings, the invasion of the
nomadic Midianites, wars with Ammon and with the
Philistines. Fortunately for Israel, a spirit of union
could still, in times of danger, be awakened among
the quarreling tribes. A brave leader, whom the Bible
calls the Judge, could rally the people in the name of
their national God. Although it seemed that after
each danger the people returned to their tribal loy-
alties as before, nevertheless, the feeling that Israel
was one people worshipping one God was slowly
making headway. The sanctuary at Shiloh, the main
seat of worship of Y, Israel's desert God, became the
meeting ground for all Israel. Out of it came Samuel,
the greatest religious teacher after Moses, who finally
laid the foundations for a united Israel. Saul's first
efforts and David's complete success at last cemented

the divided tribes into what was to become the nation of Israel.

Why did so many years pass between the time that Israel first learned from Moses the value of union and the days of Samuel when the people recognized it of their own free will? Therein lies the greatness of the leader. He understands beforehand what ordinary men will require centuries to learn through unpleasant experience.

If the people were wise, they would permit their leaders to teach them; but people are seldom wise enough. Because they lack the vision and cannot yet understand, they accuse the leaders of making conditions harder for them. How frequently the Bible tells of the Israelites' threats to kill Moses because he had taken them out of Egypt! [1]

The cooperation of the common people is further withheld because of the selfish attitude of those men at their head who would lose their power if any changes were introduced. Thus, in the days of the early settlement, if Israel were to become a united people, the local chiefs realized that they would lose their importance and power. This they bitterly resented.

The same struggle through which Israel had to pass in order to become united was experienced by all the great nations of today. England, France and Germany required hundreds of years to overcome the

[1] Exodus, chap. XVI, v. 3 and chap. XVII, v. 3

jealousies of the local nobility. The United States, too, had its war of secession. The ability to overcome sectional differences for a greater good is a sign of a nation's progress.

SUPPLEMENTARY WORK

Map Exercises

1. The fortunes of Israel change several times during this period. First Saul becomes king over a large territory of united Israel. The defeat at Gilboa and the death of Saul brings all but a small section of the country under Philistine rule. Finally David again regains the lost kingdom of Saul and increases his empire farther through extensive conquests. Let us show these changes on our maps.

On three outline maps let us shade the Kingdom of Saul at his coronation, Saul's Kingdom immediately after the defeat of Gilboa and the Empire of David at its height. Follow the maps on pages 213, 224 and 239 in your text. On each of these maps fill in the names of places which you believe important for the particular map. Of course you will include the key cities.

2. See how well you can guess: On an outline map draw again the outline of David's Empire. Shade in yellow the districts which you think would remain Israelitish always. Shade in black the districts with which the Israelites might experience difficulty.

Suggestions for Bible Study

As we suggested for section IV, you will find the interesting story paralleling this section carried further in *Into the Promised Land*, pp. 35–139.

QUESTIONS FOR THOUGHT AND DISCUSSION

1. All the nations of old have tales of heroes like our Samson stories. Why do we no longer have any such heroes today? Is there anything in modern warfare that leaves no place for heroes?
2. How would we explain the epidemic which overtook the Philistines after they brought the Ark to their cities? When do epidemics generally arise?
3. Since we do not favor kings today, should we say that the kingship was a good thing for Israel in the days of Saul and David?
4. Did Samuel act wisely in choosing a type of man like Saul?
5. Why is David considered the ideal king in Jewish history?
6. Was it right of David to take the kingship from Ishbosheth?
7. Do you know of any other case, similar to David's choice of Jerusalem, where a neutral city was selected as the national capital?

ADDITIONAL READINGS

FOR PUPILS

Hunting, *op. cit.*, pp. 73–79.

Kussy, Sarah, "In and Around Old Jerusalem," *The Young Judaean*, Vol. XIII, May, 1924, p. 7 ff.

Coffin, Helen L., "David Plays for the King," *Young Israel*, Vol. XXII, October, 1928, pp. 6–7.

Gamoran, Mamie G., "The Quest for King David"—A Legend —*Young Israel*, Vol. XVI, March, 1924, pp. 8 f.

Dubnow, S. M., *op. cit.*, Vol. I, pp. 120–170.

Lord Byron, "Song of Saul Before His Last Battle"—A Poem —*Hebrew Anthology, op. cit.*, p. 178.

Lamb, Charles & Mary, "David in the Cave of Adullam," *Hebrew Anthology*, pp. 200–201.

(Fiction)—Solis-Cohen, Emily, *David the Giant Killer*, pp. 25–42, 99–135. Philadelphia, The Jewish Publication Society of America, 1908.

Beautifully told stories, the first of David, the second of Saul and Jonathan.

Hobbs, Mabel and Mills, Helen, "David and Jonathan"—A Play—*Six Bible Plays*, pp. 97–121. New York, The Century Co., 1924.

FOR TEACHERS

Noyes, *op. cit.*, pp. 137–178.
Bailey & Kent, *op. cit.*, pp. 79–121.
Kent, *op. cit.*, pp. 138–161.
McCurdy, *op. cit.*, Vol. II, pp. 224–249.
Margolis & Marx, *op. cit.*, pp. 35–60.

Section VI

How Did Settled Life Change Our Ancestors?

Was the Conquest Worth While?

Did Israel benefit through becoming a settled nation?

Thus far we were told mainly how Israel struggled to make its possession of Canaan secure. In doing it, Israel won a place for itself among the nations of the world.

But did winning Canaan also spell progress in civilization? Two hundred years had elapsed between Joshua and the death of David. What did Israel learn of civilization during these two hundred years?

Civilization consists of many branches or departments. *One country may be more advanced in mechanics and invention, another in education, a third in its system of law, a fourth in music or painting.*

In inquiring how our ancestors progressed, we must study each department of life separately.

We must ask: Did they improve their economic condition, *that is, did they learn more skilful occupa-*

NOMADIC TENT

WORKING FOR PHARAOH

tions which repaid them better in more wholesome food, finer clothes and more comfortable dwellings?

Did they progress socially, *that is, did their relation improve toward each other and toward strangers?*

Did they grow more just *to all men and particularly did they become more kindly toward the weak and the oppressed? Did the greater justice and kindliness show itself in their system of law?*

How did settled life affect their religion? *Did the teachings of Moses flourish in the new surroundings?*

Was there any progress in general culture such as music, art, literature or education?

Did settled life make our ancestors more peaceful or more warlike?

Bear these questions in mind as you read the following section. Then try to answer to yourself:

Altogether, how far did the first two hundred years of life in Canaan carry our ancestors toward a higher civilization?

MOSES   PLOUGHING IN CANAAN

How Did Settled Life Change Our Ancestors?

PART I

WE HAVE followed the story of our ancestors' growth into a nation from the period of desert wandering to the successful founding of an Israelitish empire in the Westland by King David. Living for centuries among unknown desert tribes, Israel finally appears on the scene of recorded history as the slave of the Egyptian Pharaoh. The great Moses leads the separate tribes from Egypt, teaches them a new religion and attempts to mold them into one people. After several hundred years of trial and struggle, of victory and defeat, Israel has at last achieved one goal of its journey. It is already a unified nation, living in its own land with but a single government. It has climbed a few rungs on the ladder of civilization.

SETTLEMENT IN NEW COUNTRY PRODUCES CHANGES

The ways of life of a whole people can be changed only very slowly. Human beings like to continue their occupations, their habits of eating, sleeping, talking

251

or worshipping. However, when they come to a new country where other customs are observed, they begin to feel somewhat uncomfortable in their old habits. That is especially true if the older inhabitants of the land are better educated, wealthier or in other ways more advanced than the newcomers.

The poor immigrant, for example, who comes to the United States from a small European village, wishes to retain as many of his former practices as he can, desiring at the same time, however, to become thoroughly Americanized. As a result there is a mixture of the two civilizations. In some respects he becomes American, while in others he remains as he was in Europe.

Thus, he will most readily exchange his former occupation for one at which he can earn more. He will soon move to a modern comfortable apartment and furnish it with the best American household goods that he can afford.

Religious beliefs, on the other hand, or ideas of right and wrong, of what is moral or immoral, will change least readily. While there may be a few who will easily cast off their ancient beliefs and ideals for those that they find in the new land, the large majority refuses for many years to give up any of them. Several generations may have to pass before the European is willing to compare his beliefs and ideals with those of his fellow Americans to find the truth that is in both.

Israelites Newcomers to Canaanite Civilization

Our ancestors upon their settlement in Canaan were, like the immigrant to this country, newcomers to a civilization richer than any to which they had till then been accustomed. The differences between nomadic and settled life are great and, as we have suggested, changes did not take place equally rapidly in all departments. Some nomadic habits were given up early. In the days of the Judges most of the Israelites were already farmers and lived in houses instead of tents, though some clans permanently preferred tent dwelling and sheeptending. Changes in government or religious beliefs, on the other hand, were slow and difficult to bring about. We should expect life in Canaan during the period of King David to represent a mixture of settled life with remains of nomadic elements. Some changes would be of unquestioned good, making life happier and better, while others might be not so beneficial, and in some cases even harmful. Wherein did settled life prove of absolute advantage to our ancestors? In which respects was it only partially good? Did it in any ways bring evil together with the good? We shall consider the answers to these questions in the present section.

Before we start, we must give a word of warning which we shall repeat frequently. Even settled life in ancient times was very far from what it is today.

During the past two centuries the world has in many departments made such great progress that the cities, houses and farms even of settled peoples would hardly appeal to us as places in which to live. However, if we picture a people climbing toward a higher place in the world, we shall understand how great the advance is from nomadism to settled life.

IMPROVED CONDITIONS—VARIETY OF OCCUPATIONS

The most rapid changes and those of greatest benefit produced upon our ancestors by settled life were in the manner of earning a livelihood. We recall that nomads are skilled in very few occupations, which are simply divided into the work of the men and the work of the women. The men tend the flocks, slaughter animals for food, and work with the tanned hides. The women cook, bake, spin and make the tents.

Learn Agriculture

Now our wandering ancestors found themselves in a land where the ground yielded yearly harvests, where there was rich and plentiful grass for the flocks, and water was abundant throughout the year. Wherever the soil was good for agriculture, the shepherd nomads readily took to farming. Agriculture was more profitable than cattle grazing, and promised a more steady supply of food. The hilly

PLOUGHING

Today, as in ancient times, the poor Fellah (Arab farmer) follows
his slow oxen behind a wooden plow as the Canaanite farmer did
three thousand years before him.

country of Ephraim was covered with corn and barley and with vegetable gardens. The rich Plain of
Esdraelon and the fertile shores of Chinnereth produced wheat. The rocky slopes of Judah abounded
in olive groves and thousands of trailing vines. All
these the Canaanites had planted before them; and
the Israelites, making slaves of the Canaanites,
forced them to continue their labors.

In the south of Judah, in Gilead, and in places in
Ephraim and Galilee, many families continued their

TREADING GRAPES TODAY

Today the grapes are thrown into a box and barefoot men tread them as in olden times. A jar below the box catches the juice.

former nomadic habits and occupations. The lowing of the herds could still be heard in the land. To the very end of the existence of the kingdom many such families chose to remain tenders of sheep. The greater part of the nation, however, was engaged in farming, and in the days of King David, Israel was an agricultural nation.

The farmer of old did not have all the aids which science now offers him. He had no chemical fertilizer to improve his fields. His plough was not of fine steel which cuts deep furrows, but of wood tipped with bronze or stone, which only scratched the surface soil. He had no gasoline tractor to draw it, nor even horses, but only slow-plodding oxen. For other tools, such as hoes and sickles, the Canaanite farmer used flint and rarely bronze, where we use iron.

Farming operations, in general, were very simple. After the grain was cut, it was spread on a sacred rock for threshing. The operation was performed either by driving oxen over the stalks to beat the grains out of the husks with their hoofs or by drawing sledges over them. The grain was then thrown up to let the wind carry away the chaff. Even such important tasks as the preparation of wine and oil were done very crudely. The grapes were thrown into a vat cut out of the solid rock, and men treaded them with the feet to press out the juice. Olives were cared for a little more delicately by pressing on them with a beam. In either case the process was slow and

WINE-PRESS

The ancient wine-press was a large, square hole or vat cut into the solid rock. The grapes were then thrown in and men jumped over them to press out the juice. A channel was cut to connect up with a lower vat into which the juice flowed.

hardly thorough. The income from farming was therefore far below what farms produce today. However, in comparison with the nomad, even the ancient farmer was prosperous.

Beginnings in Handicrafts

The farmer needed tools and implements, a plough, a hoe, a pitchfork and a scythe. When tools became dull, they needed sharpening. The farmer's wife needed pots and pans. At first the Israelite farmer was obliged to go to the Canaanite handworker in the city, to the blacksmith, the potter or the tanner. Soon some Israelites preferred handicrafts to herding sheep or farming. They learned the trade from the Canaanites and set up their own shops. Now one was able to find occasional Israelite potters, blacksmiths, makers of weapons, coppersmiths and tanners.

The new Israelitish handworkers were not yet skilful enough to make fine articles. The pottery of this period, for example, is of coarse clay, carelessly made, unevenly fired and very poorly decorated. For many years skilled workmen were brought in from other countries, particularly from Phoenicia. When King David wanted a palace built for himself, he imported workmen from Phoenicia, and we shall see

ANCIENT HEBREW POTTERY

These three pieces found at Jericho and Megiddo are examples of finer wares which were either imported from the Greek Island of Cyprus or else were copied from imported models. The early original Hebrew pottery was very crude.

later that the famous Temple of Solomon likewise was built by mechanics from that land. Costly wares might also be bought on market days from the passing caravans. It was from these foreign craftsmen and merchants that Israel was learning the finer and more artistic occupations in which in time it, too, would be able to engage. This was Israel's introduction to the world of beautiful things.

ADVANTAGE OF NEW OCCUPATIONS OVER NOMADIC LIFE

Let us again remember, as we read of the great changes which took place among our ancestors, not to imagine that they were wealthy and prosperous in the same way that people are wealthy and prosperous today. Much of the land was not what we would consider very fertile. The Israelite farmer and his family had to work very hard to earn a livelihood. The Bible describes working for a living by the expression, "In the sweat of thy face shalt thou eat bread." [1] Men still toiled from dawn to sunset and women ground the flour, spun the flax and wool, made mats, cooked, baked, and often rose even before their husbands to complete their many tasks. There were years when the rains were not sufficient so that the land suffered from drought and famine, of which the Bible occasionally makes mention. The

[1] Genesis, chap. III, v. 19

same causes which forced Jacob and his sons to migrate to Egypt continued at times to work great
hardship among the poor of the land. In after years
we read of the great drought in the days of King
David. However, when we compare settled life with
that of nomads who face famine all the time, never
certain of tomorrow's bread, we can understand the
improvement in the fortunes of our ancestors.

Improvement in Settlement and Shelter

Just as this period was Israel's introduction to agriculture with handicrafts, so it was the beginning of

A GATE IN THE WALLS OF JERUSALEM

The older part of Jerusalem still has a wall about it with gates
and towers. The present wall is about four hundred years old.

life in cities and villages. Nomads lived in encamp-
ments, camps where tents are pitched for as long a
time as the tribe finds it safe or convenient to remain.
The nomadic camp is open to attack by raiders or
wild animals. The nomadic tent is poor shelter
against sun, cold or storm. The city or village is a
place where a person hopes to spend his entire life.
Therefore he can make himself a home that will
shelter him better than the nomadic tent, and he can
protect it better by building fortifications around his
entire village or city. Let us proceed to get a picture
of the homes and cities in which our ancestors were
now to live.

THE CITY

Great and important as was the change from the
encampment to the city, we must yet remember that
the city and village of ancient times, or even of the
Middle Ages, were more like an encampment than
like anything we call a city today. Should an aviator
have flown over an ancient city, he would have described it as a collection of mud or stone huts, with
a few crooked, muddy lanes swarming with men and
animals. Few cities covered an area of more than
one by two large city blocks.

Yet the city was a great advance over the open
camp. The city was the walled residence of the surrounding farmers and the few tradespeople and hand-

workers who attended to their needs. The city was also the place where men could trade and get manufactured articles or where they could gather to witness interesting happenings. The two most important features of the ancient city were, its encircling massive walls and the marketplace at the gate.

The Walls

The city walls were of stone and so thick that often two carriages could pass each other on the top. In the walls there were gates which were opened in the morning and closed at night, except in time of war. Near the gate was a high watch tower on which guards were always posted to warn of an approaching enemy. A very large city, such as Jerusalem later became, had several gates and towers situated at the various roads leading into it. Even today one may still see an example of a city wall around the old city of Jerusalem. This, however, is a modern wall, having been built only a few hundred years ago.

The Marketplace

The second important part of the city was the marketplace, which was situated at the gate. In this open space, everything of importance in the city took place. Merchants, artisans and farmers from the country came to the gate to sell their wares, and sales of fields and houses were completed there. However, the marketplace was also put to other uses. There the town crier made his important announcements, and often teachers, prophets and other speakers addressed the people. Since all business was transacted in the marketplace, it might be expected that there also most of the quarrels would arise. The court was, therefore, held at the gate, as well as the legislative councils; and the judges are often called "those who sit at the gate." Chairs were generally placed for the elders, and in later times a platform was erected for them. Thus, whenever a case came before the judges, all the citizens might gather about to listen. All strangers naturally found their way to the marketplace first, and if they were unsuccessful in receiving the hospitality of some kindly citizen, they might be obliged to sleep in the open. Games, dances, celebrations and military exhibitions, all the business, all the government and all the pleasures of the people were centered at the gate.

Streets and Shops

The rest of the city, like Arab cities today, like European cities several centuries ago, consisted of a few narrow lanes, so narrow that a camel walking in the middle of the street with packs on his sides might have these set on fire from a light burning inside a shop. Of course, the streets were not paved,

A SPICE SHOP IN ARABIC PALESTINE

Notice that the shop is small and most of the wares are outside. In olden times the store was even smaller and practically all the trading took place out-of-doors.

and in the rainy season they were almost impassable. Sidewalks were unknown, and men and beasts shared the narrow alleys. Some streets were occupied almost entirely by the handworkers. These had tiny dark shops; and, therefore, they preferred to do their work or to sell their wares outside in front of their shops. In the old Arab cities in Palestine life today is as it was thousands of years ago, and one can still find the Arab vendors squatting in front of their shops with all their goods and tools about them.

THE HOME AND ITS FURNISHINGS

In the other streets lived the townspeople. Let us take a peep into their homes for only a moment, for possibly we should not care to remain much longer.

The home of the average city-dweller consisted of a
courtyard and a house. The courtyard was four-
cornered, and the house was situated in one of the
corners. The house seemed to stand with its back to
the street, the outer wall containing neither door nor
windows—these were within the courtyard. The
dwelling consisted of one room about ten feet wide
and twelve or fifteen feet long. The floor was divided
into two parts, one lower and the other a little raised
and reached by a short ladder. In the lower part of
the room the animals were lodged for the night; in the
higher section lived the people of the house. In
the center of the dwelling was the hearth, for the
fire. The smoke had to escape as best it could through
the door or the window opening. There was usually
but one small window, built high in the wall to keep
out the hot sun. Glass was a luxury used only by

HOME VERSUS TENT

Even the mud pile which represented the home of the poor
peasant was far more comfortable than the former nomadic tent.

ON THE ROOF

the very wealthy. In the average home a wooden shutter closed the opening on cold or stormy days. The roof was made of grass and mud, a mixture which did not always successfully withstand the terrible downpours of the rainy season.

The furniture of the house was at first as simple as that of the tent. People sat, ate and slept on mats. We shall see how in time the richer homes introduced chairs, tables, beds and costly rugs which the foreign merchants brought to the country. The walls were decorated with weapons, animal heads or horns.

There was only one comfortable spot in the house, the roof. This was flat, and was reached by a ladder from the outside. Usually a breastwork was built around it to prevent people from falling off. On the roof, the family performed many of its tasks, the women doing their work there toward evening, the men conversing and arranging the family worship. Persons of means built a guest chamber on the roof.

The house was not thought of as a place in which to live, as we use it today. It was merely a shelter against the sun by day and the cold by night. Men came home only to eat or to sleep; otherwise they spent the rest of their time in the open.

CITY AND DWELLINGS—A SUMMARY

Such was the city, and such were the dwellings of our ancestors at the time of their settlement in

Canaan; and so they remained with little change till the destruction of the kingdom. Later the nobles built larger houses with more rooms or of more than one story. The average citizen continued in the same simple dwelling. If a son married and there was no room for him within the house, another house was built in another corner of the court. The house was rudely put together with uneven stones and mud, little care being taken to fit the stones one to another or to build the wall solidly. It was not at all unusual, therefore, for holes to remain in the wall, and often dangerous serpents made their home there. Nor was it unusual for homes to tumble down during storms.

Why did people live in such small, crowded, stuffy houses when with a little effort they might have been more comfortable? We must remember what these people had been accustomed to. Imagine yourself caught in a violent storm on a lonely road or exposed to the desert sun. How you would welcome any shelter, even if it were nothing more than a ruined house or abandoned barn! The desert peoples had borne the fierce rays of the sun in their hot tents. On frosty nights and during the rainy season they had suffered in their weak shelters. What if their present house was crowded and the roof did leak a bit!

We have thus seen the progress that Israel made in its way of living. From nomadic life, in which they were always threatened with lack of food and water, they turned to agriculture and were, therefore, much more certain of earning a livelihood. The land was not the most fertile in the world, and men had to work hard; but life now was a great improvement over what it had been. It provided a greater variety of foods. It brought in such luxuries as oil, for anointing the body, and wine which "delighteth the heart of man." It opened up many new occupations to a people which heretofore had known but few. The kind of shelter which the people now used was better, and this resulted in improved health and longer life. Above all, the new way of living made for greater safety and security, so that the minds of a few of the better men could turn from wars and dangers to peace and to human brotherhood.

Advantages That Also Brought Disadvantage

The changes we have described thus far were entirely to the advantage of our ancestors; but settled agricultural life itself introduced modification in the relations among the members of the clans. Would these, too, be entirely for the better? In the main we should answer "Yes," for as a result of living in cities and villages, members of the clans would become more concerned with the welfare of the entire country rather than with the welfare merely of their own fellow clansmen. However, in the process of change, something was lost, also.

The democratic equality of nomadic life was disappearing. Wealth and poverty were no longer shared, but every person looked after his own interests. Accordingly, there developed differences in wealth and social standing. There were now poor and rich, slave and nobleman. Let us see how life as farmers influenced the ancient clan organization.

Blood Relationship Versus Neighborhood

You recall that, when we first made the acquaintance of our ancestors, they were living as clans or large families. Several of these enlarged families or clans belonged to one tribe; and these tribes, too, had a feeling of relationship among themselves. The clan had its own government through the patriarch. It worshipped its own god, it made its own laws, and protected its fellow-members through the sacred duty of blood revenge. The constant danger of attack and the search for food in bands drew the members closely together, so that they looked upon each other as brothers.

Such an organization, which must have existed among the nomads for hundreds, perhaps thousands of years, would certainly be very slow to change. Even hundreds of years after they entered the land some clans remained as they had been during the period of their desert wandering. A person still needed the protection of the clan, for, though now the elders might give judgment in the case of wrongs committed, there was as yet no one to enforce the judgment aside from the relatives of the injured person. Settled life made necessary many changes in organization and government, which tended to weaken the hold of the clan upon its members.

Members No Longer Share Wealth

The most important change which settled life caused in the nomadic clan was to make each of its members, rather than the clan as a whole, responsible for his daily needs. Although at first the land may have been assigned to the clan as a whole, in time it was broken up into shares which the smaller family within the clan tilled for itself. The holding of common property was passing out of use, and each family was obliged to provide for itself.

Must Join With Neighbors for Protection—Patriotism

The need for protection, which, as we have noted, is the strongest bond of union in nomadic life, was now satisfied in a different manner. A person was still dependent on his blood relatives to avenge an injustice to himself. Thus, if a person received hurt to his body, all members of his clan would avenge him. If a man was killed, his clan would seek blood revenge. However, there were now occasions when the protection of the clan proved insufficient, namely, in time of war or raids. Nomads usually fight in small groups, composed of raiding parties which can easily run away. Settled people cannot run away from their settlement. They must protect their homes against invaders, and for such protection they need larger armies than single clans. Thus, when a village is attacked by a foreign army, its own members alone are hardly sufficient to repel an invasion. At best, the several hundred fighting men which the clan might muster form only one small company in the thousands of troops needed for a war of settled peoples. The manhood of the entire tribe is not sufficient: it must seek union with other tribes. The clan thus probably still fights as a unit under its own chiefs, providing its own equipment and commissary; but it recognizes that it is no longer the largest group to which its members owe allegiance. It has become a sub-unit of the larger group, the entire nation. The nation is no longer a family group of persons related to one another. It consists of many persons sharing a common land. In order to retain their land, all men must be willing to defend their neighbors' property as well as their own, regardless of whether their neighbors belong to their own clan or to a different one. The relation of neighbor thus in time becomes almost as important as that of blood relative. Loyalty to clan begins to give way to love and loyalty for country. This we now call "patriotism."

Power of Patriarch Limited to Village Government

Everything in settled life forces people to move out of their narrow groups into a wider world. The more important governmental powers of the patriarchs are taken over by the king, and to the former chiefs is left the post of village heads or city elders. The more powerful among them are made generals and nobles by the king; but it is the king's government which is supreme. The result is that many former privileges of the clan-father as well as of the clan itself are restricted. When we read of the laws of the time we shall see that, while a disobedient son or one who insulted his parents might still be severely punished, the judges had to decide upon the punishment and not, as formerly, the head of the household. Even the sacred duty of blood revenge was forbidden in certain cases. The separate families might no longer take justice into their own hands. Thus the weakening of the clan, too, is a sign of growth.

THE DISADVANTAGES—GROWTH OF SOCIAL CLASSES

We saw that settled life and the weakening of the clan helped Israel to reach out into a greater world; but, in accepting the benefits of settlement and civilization, Israel was forced to lose some of the finer elements of nomadic life.

The nomadic clan is like a large family. Everyone works and receives his food and clothing in return. When the tribe has no food, everyone is hungry, but when food is plentiful, all share it. The desert-dweller, who is prepared to divide his morsel with the stranger, can certainly be trusted to care for his brother.

We find, therefore, that within the early clan all members are alike. No one is rich, and no one is poor. If any man is honored more than another, it is for his great strength or bravery in war.

After Israel settled in cities and villages and turned to tilling the soil, its life underwent a change in this respect. No longer did all wealth belong to the patriarch, who was to share it among the members of the clan. Every man was assigned his own plot of ground, from which he was to earn his livelihood. When a man ploughed and sowed or when he gathered in his harvest, he thought only of what it would yield for his own household. If his neighbor proved to be less fortunate, he might be sorry for him and help him, as we do our needy relatives, but that depended upon his choice. Fellow-clansmen were drawing apart, were being regarded more as neighbors than relatives. One person might have too much, while another starved: the more prosperous person was no longer expected to share his goods with his unsuccessful neighbor. There were now rich and poor in Israel.

How Inequalities Arose

Whether the land was originally divided among the
clans or among single families within the clan we
do not know. Nor do we know whether all families
received equal shares according to the number of
their members, or whether the more powerful families
received larger portions. It was natural that after a
number of years some farmers would be more successful than others. The soil might be better in one
village than in another, or one farmer might be more
skilful or more thrifty. As we noted before, there
were years of drought when there was no rain and no
harvest. The richer farmer could save enough during
the good years to tide him over times of shortage;
but the poorer man had nothing on which to live
during periods of famine. He was obliged to borrow
money which he could never hope to repay except
through the sale of his field and his home, and that
forced him to hire himself out as a laborer.

Going to work at that time was not as it is today.
In those days there were not many working men
who worked for wages. A farmer might hire himself
out for a day or two, if his own farm did not require
all his time. Handworkers often hired out their services for the day or for a special piece of work. However, the great majority of laborers were slaves,
Canaanites or other prisoners taken in the many

wars. It was cheaper for the Israelite to buy a Canaanite slave than to hire a Hebrew workingman. The Israelite who wanted work had but one choice left—to sell himself as a slave. Often the choice was forced upon him. If he owed a debt and could not pay it, his debtor might sell not only him, but his sons and daughters. The only escape from such slavery was to live the life of an outlaw, as the men did who made up David's band when he fled from Saul.

The quality which existed within the clan thus began to disappear. In its place was laid the foundation for social classes. There were the beginnings of rich and poor, freemen and slaves, each looking with suspicion and hatred upon the other. Israelite could no longer call Israelite brother, for within one's own clan there was apt to be the man who might use the misfortunes of his neighbor to his own advantage. We shall see, as we continue our study, that these conditions grew worse. There was an increasing number of rich landowners possessing large estates and of poor persons who owned little.

Social Changes Come Very Slowly

Important, though, as were the changes which were taking place, they came about very slowly. The clan remained both outwardly and within much as it had been before. Although caring for independent households, the large family with its dependents and slaves still clung together, generally living in the same village, even though some of the members were scattered. The majority of the people lived on farms, where the old ways of life continued in their same form for many years. The head of the clan, the household father, was now the village elder, and still retained most of the authority of the patriarch, though his power was not as absolute as it had been. Abusing one's father or mother was as treasonable as it later became to insult the king, and might be punished with great severity. The father still had control over his sons and daughters and had the power to arrange marriages for them. Even those members of the clan who lived away from home were still subject to the control of the clan and assembled at certain important occasions for the family offerings.

Accordingly we must keep in mind that change comes quietly, almost unnoticed. A clan was no longer an independent self-governing unit; but formed a small village or even part of a village. Of these there now existed thousands in Israel. The transformation was a great one indeed, though the average Israelitish householder would hardly have admitted that anything new had happened within his family in the two or three hundred years of life in Canaan. Life is always modified, but so slowly that we seldom notice the change.

A SUMMARY PICTURE

Before discussing further changes in the life of Israel, let us pause for a moment to form a picture of our ancestors as they lived in their own homeland. Some were to be found in cities, but most of them had their homes in villages. They continued living in clans or large families very much as in nomadic days. The old equality, however, was disappearing. There were now rich and poor, and even Israelitish slaves. With the growth of the kingship, a new class was arising, which because of distinguished service or merely because it enjoyed royal favor, was selected for nobility and other special privileges. The captives of war and those who willingly surrendered themselves, such as the Gibeonites, formed a large slave popula-

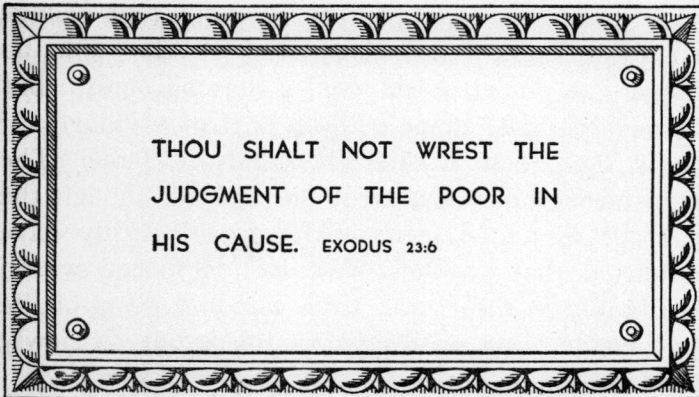

> THOU SHALT NOT WREST THE JUDGMENT OF THE POOR IN HIS CAUSE. EXODUS 23:6

tion. The Canaanites, the former inhabitants of the
land, were either made slaves or, frequently, were
admitted as equals into the nation of Israel, since
they could hardly be distinguished from the Israelites in language, dress or appearance. All the groups
whom we have mentioned, together with merchants
from strange lands and passing travelers, non-
Hebrews who were adopted into Israelite families,
formed the population of the land of Israel.

CHANGES IN LAW AND JUSTICE

Changes in life are like the links of a chain——one
link must fit into the other. We saw how new occupations brought a change in social classes. What
changes would new social classes bring about? A
people which was accustomed to equality found itself
divided into groups of differing privilege. It became
necessary to protect the poor and the weak and to
curb the power of the strong. Settled life, therefore,
led to progress in law and justice. This was not only
an advantage to our ancestors but the beginning of
a great achievement which was to benefit mankind.

Lex Talionis Modified

When we spoke of justice in nomadic times, you may
recall, we mentioned the "Lex Talionis," the law
which required a person to repay in exactly the same

form any action or injury he had suffered from another. We spoke also of Blood Revenge, the duty of all members of the family to avenge an injury to any of their number.

These ideas were continued in settled life as well. Even today we find the *vendetta* or feud in the mountain districts of some of the states of our country. The practice of one nation going to war against another because of an injury to one of its citizens is in a modified form a continuation of the blood feud. Every step away from the blood feud and from the *Lex Talionis* is of the greatest importance in the story of mankind, as the *Lex Talionis* itself was an advance over more ancient justice. It is especially interesting to us as Jews to see how our own people, when they had settled, began to rise above the old nomadic ways of dealing out justice.

LAW OF DAMAGES

In the Book of Exodus, there is a section (Chapter XXI) which begins with the words, "Now these are the ordinances which thou shalt set before them!" It is believed that these were the laws of Israel at the period of history which we are studying, or possibly a little later. These laws still recognize the right of the avenger of blood to slay the murderer of his relative, and it appears that other members of the household continue to share the criminal's guilt.

The family of the injured person, too, is as yet the only authority for enforcing the law, there being no governmental police force. The *Lex Talionis* is as yet the law of the tribes. The code declares "Eye for eye, tooth for tooth, hand for hand, foot for foot, burning for burning."

The step in advance, however, is that the penalties are not to be applied in every case. The *Lex Talionis* is to be used only when a lasting injury results to the eye, hand, foot, etc. If the hurt can be cured, the *Lex Talionis* is no longer enforced. A new idea of justice is introduced, which we follow to this day: the injured person is paid in money for the damage he has suffered. We now call this payment "damages." Our ancestors were already beginning to see that it does little good to the injured man to have the person who caused the injury hurt in the same way. Whenever possible, the law code now substituted a fine for a body punishment. It was extended to all cases where a man's property did the damages, as, for example, where his ox killed a person or where his fire burned the house or vineyard of another.

Poor, Widow, Orphan and Stranger Protected

We saw how the changed conditions within the clan created new social classes, dividing the people into rich and poor. The plight of the poor caused our ancestors great concern. They still had the tradition

IF THOU AT ALL TAKE THY NEIGH-
BOUR'S GARMENT TO PLEDGE, THOU
SHALT RESTORE IT UNTO HIM BY THAT
THE SUN THAT GOETH DOWN.

EXODUS 22:25

of a time when the goods of the tribe were shared by all alike. Now that inequality was arising, the rich were commanded to deal kindly with the poor. If a poor man borrows money, he must not be charged interest. If he gives his cloak as a pledge, it must be returned to him every night, since otherwise he might have no covering. Every seven years the fields must be left fallow, and all that grows of itself without planting must be offered freely to the poor. In like manner, one must be kind to the widow and the orphan, who have lost their natural protector, or to the stranger who has no friends. The code continues that, if any of these provisions are not observed and the oppressed cry to God, severe punishment will be visited by God for such violation. Since all rights were enforced by the relatives or family of the injured person, widows, orphans and strangers, having no protectors, were dependent upon the care of God himself.

Rights of Slaves Declared

Of special interest are the laws dealing with slaves, because in these we can see how far the feeling of humanity was developed among our ancestors. We may better understand the spirit of our old slave laws, if we bear in mind the cruel manner in which slaves were treated in all ages from ancient times down to the last century in our own country.

Strange as the idea may sound to us today, slavery in ancient time was an act of kindness. Slaves were captives of war, whose lives were spared. The story of the Gibeonites in the book of Joshua [1] is a very fine example of this practice, and shows how rarely prisoners of war were saved from execution. Among the surrounding peoples, slaves enjoyed very few rights, their masters having the power of life and death over them. However, our ancestors were constantly reminded that, since they, too, had been slaves and strangers in Egypt, they must have compassion for the slave. In this code of laws alone we find the warning and the reminder repeated twice. The limitations put upon the rights of the master in dealing with his slave is thus another measure of progress.

[1] Chap. IX

> AND IF A MAN SMITE HIS BONDMAN,
> OR HIS BONDWOMAN, WITH A ROD, AND
> HE DIE UNDER HIS HAND, HE SHALL
> SURELY BE PUNISHED. EXODUS 21:20

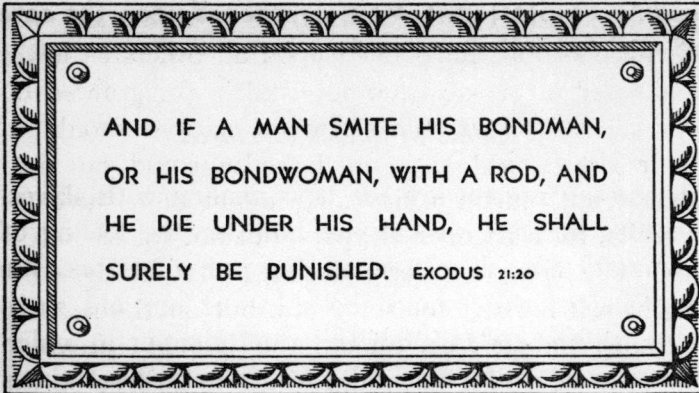

The most significant change in the law concerning slaves was that of making the master subject to punishment for killing his slave. We can see what an advance this was in common practice by the fact that even this law makes an exception of cases where the slave lives a few days after the injuries are inflicted. We thus see how hard it was to make people understand that a slave is a human being and not property. Further laws state that if a master injures a slave seriously, the slave thereby gains his freedom. The law also commands the master to allow the slave one day of rest during the week.

HEBREW SLAVES

A distinction is made in the treatment of heathen and of Hebrew slaves. We have noted how ancient peoples considered their own tribe or nation the only civilized people and looked upon all others as lower and inferior. It was, therefore, taken for granted by our ancestors that men of foreign nations should be their slaves, but that an Israelite could not and should not remain a slave. He might be a slave for a while, for a number of years, but not for his whole life. The law, therefore, declares that an Israelite might sell himself for six years, but on the seventh he must be set free. Should the Israelite prove to have the soul of a slave and refuse to go free on the seventh year, his ear is to be bored with an awl as a sign of disgrace: after that he might remain a slave forever.

If a man bought a Hebrew girl slave, it was generally understood that he or his son would marry her. If this condition was not fulfilled, she had to

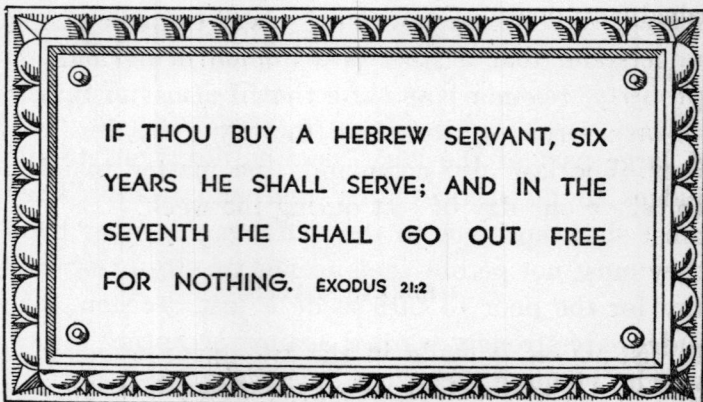

IF THOU BUY A HEBREW SERVANT, SIX YEARS HE SHALL SERVE; AND IN THE SEVENTH HE SHALL GO OUT FREE FOR NOTHING. EXODUS 21:2

AND HE THAT STEALETH A MAN, AND
SELLETH HIM, OR IF HE BE FOUND IN
HIS HAND, HE SHALL SURELY BE PUT
TO DEATH. EXODUS 21:16

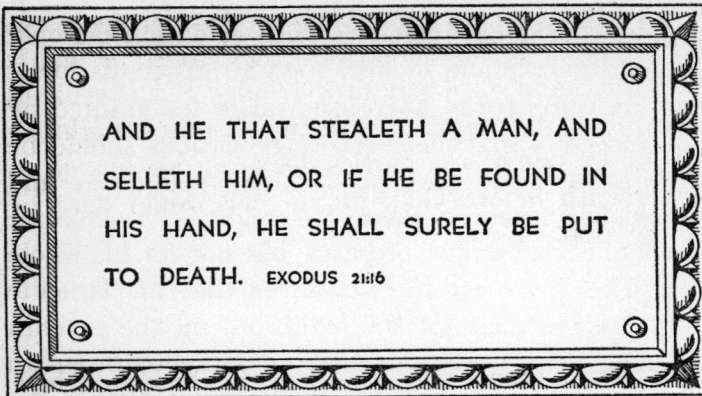

be set free when she became of age.

Because of the very large slave trade in ancient times, it was customary for raiding parties to fall upon peaceful villages and kidnap persons for sale into slavery. This practice is very strongly condemned and a person guilty of kidnapping was punished with death.

Conduct of Judges Prescribed

A large part of the laws contains directions to the judges to do justice fairly and impartially. They must show no favor to the rich; on the other hand they must not permit their feeling of pity or sympathy for the poor to turn aside a just decision. The judges are strongly warned against accepting bribes, which "blindeth them that have sight."

The judges are called *Elohim*, God, or representatives of God. For that reason they are to be highly respected, and an insult to the judge is an insult to God whom he represents. Many disputes might be settled by one of the parties declaring his innocence under oath before God, for no one would dare lie before God.

Other Laws

There are a number of other laws in the code which are of interest to us. The three festivals—of unleavened bread, of the first fruits, and of the final ingathering—are here commanded. It is also commanded that on these three occasions all males appear before the Lord by making a pilgrimage to the place where the Ark of the Covenant was kept. The law also declares what Israelites may not eat, and thus furnishes the basis for the dietary laws of later periods. "Thou shalt not seethe a kid in its mother's milk" has been explained to forbid our eating milk and meat together. The command not to eat the meat of beasts found slain in the field has grown into the regulations for slaughtering animals in a definitely prescribed manner.

Special gifts to God are ordered, among them the sacrifice of the first born of man or animal to God. Among primitive peoples a child may actually have been offered up, but we find a very early protest in

THE CODE OF HAMMURABI

This picture shows the top of a tall stone monument on which is inscribed the famous Babylonian law code. This picture shows King Hammurabi receiving the laws from Shamash, the Sun God.

Israel against such a practice. The story of the sacrifice of Isaac tells that God does not want human sacrifice. Another gift was, therefore, substituted in place of the child, a custom which has remained among us to this day in the form of *"Pidyon ha-Ben,"* the ceremony in which the father of the first born son redeems him from the Kohen (priest).

The Law—A Sign of Progress

The study of the Laws clearly shows a forward movement on the part of our ancestors. There is a spirit of kindliness and justice in all of these laws. This code or Book of the Covenant, as it is called, has often been compared with a famous Babylonian code of laws, called the Laws of Hammurabi. We do find many of the Hebrew laws very much like the older Babylonian code. The organization of the code, too, shows that its authors were familiar with the Babylonian laws. Yet there are some very important differences. The Laws of Hammurabi are much more severe in the punishment of crime than are the Hebrew Laws. Stealing and like offenses are punished by death in the Babylonian code. The failure to return an escaped slave is punished in the same manner, whereas the Israelite laws forbid returning a fugitive slave. The Babylonian law is concerned mainly with protecting the property rights of the rich, while our ancient Hebrew law is interested rather in safeguarding the rights of persons who, because of poverty, bondage or death of their protector, cannot defend their own rights.

Yet again we must not fail to notice how slowly the mind of man changes. The *Lex Talionis* is modified, but not completely abolished, while the blood feud still persists. A slave may not be killed at will. On the other hand, if he is attacked by his master and he lives a day or two after his injury the master is not punished. Moreover, we cannot be certain that all the laws listed in the code were actually enforced by the government. Some of them may represent the ideal of the religious teachers rather than the practice of the judge. Yet even where the code merely suggests laws to the lawmaker, it is the beginning of those ideas which are the seeds of what we describe as progress and civilization.

PART II

CHANGES IN RELIGION—LARGELY DISADVANTAGEOUS

NOT all changes which Israel underwent in Canaan, as we have seen, were to the advantage of our ancestors. The benefits derived from the new methods of earning a livelihood were somewhat offset by the growth of social classes. This, however, led to the higher development of law. Similarly the new agricultural interests brought about changes in religious practices which led to a finer religion among some small groups, but had the opposite effect on the majority of Israel.

When we speak of the religion of our ancestors, let us not imagine that all held identical beliefs, which can be described as the religion of Israel. Such a condition never exists among any people. A nation is always composed of several layers; the lowest clings to a religion of superstitions, a middle group is ready to follow those in authority, and the highest layer strives for a purer religion. The lowest layer is always the largest, while the smallest number is found in the highest group. Even today the religion of the most ignorant part of our community is altogether different from that of the higher groups.

We must, therefore, study each group separately to understand how life in Canaan influenced the religion of our ancestors.

THE LOWEST LAYER IMITATES CANAANITES

The lowest layer among the Israelites copied the religion of the Canaanites—and quite naturally so. The Canaanite was not entirely a stranger to the Hebrew, since both Canaanite and Hebrew spoke the same language and resembled each other in many respects. Of the two peoples the Canaanites were the more advanced in civilization, the Israelites feeling rather ignorant and helpless before them. All the new skills needed for life in Canaan had to be learned from the Canaanites. The Canaanite taught the Hebrew how to plough, plant or thresh. The Canaanite, too, taught him to build homes, make pots, work in iron, or eat and sleep in more civilized fashion. In similar manner the Canaanite taught the new settlers about the gods of the land and how to do them honor.

Canaanite Religion Agricultural

The character of the Canaanitish religion made it particularly natural for the Hebrews to learn it readily. The Canaanite religion was a farming religion, which every farmer was expected to know as part of his knowledge of agriculture. We today generally separate work from worship. When the day's work is done or on days when we do not work, we gather at our synagogues to pray to God. In ancient times certain forms of worship were included among the steps necessary in performing a given task. The Canaanite farmer, for example, in describing how a crop is planted, might tell the Hebrew first to plough, then to sacrifice and sow his seeds, after which it might be important to go through a magic dance of prayer for rain. For the Canaanite the sacrifice was as essential to the success of the crop as the placing of seeds in the ground. The simple Hebrew farmer, as an obedient pupil would faithfully follow all the instructions given him.

God Called Baal

Accordingly the religion of the lowest layer of the Israelites was the religion of the Canaanite peasants. The Canaanites worshipped gods called *"Baal"* (owner) whom they considered the owners of their fields. The *Baal* was mainly interested in the fertility of the soil, in the weather, and in the sun and moon which influence the weather. Each *Baal* was believed to have a wife, *Baala,* or more generally called *Ashtoroth* or *Astarte*. The main symbol of the *Baal* was the *Mazebah,* or pillar of stone, and of the goddess, a tree called in Hebrew the *Asherah*. Besides

ASTARTE

These small Canaanite images of the female goddess or Baala were found in the diggings at Taanach.

the *Baal,* other gods were worshipped, particularly *Tammuz,* also called *Adon* (lord or master), a name which in later Greek was changed to *Adonis.* The legend of *Tammuz,* the god of plants and flowers, was that every autumn the god was snatched away to the lower world, so that all plants and flowers died. His mother, *Astarte,* would then go in search of him and would bring him to earth again in the early spring. *Tammuz* was worshipped, therefore, by the planting of flower gardens in the spring and by wailing for his passing in the early autumn.

Gods Local—Worshipped Through Images

We can thus see how the Israelites who accepted Baal worship went back to a lower form of religion. They abandoned the worship of the God of Moses, the mightiest of gods, who would not permit His worshippers to share His worship with lesser gods. Instead the Israelites now returned to a belief in a small district god, one of many, who was in no way distinguished from, and in many respects less important than the great gods of Babylon or Egypt. No longer did they pay heed to the command against making pictures or images of the gods. While few large images have been found in the excavations carried on in Palestine, those that have been unearthed show that *Baal* was often represented as a bull-god, though it is not clear whether the bull was intended as the god himself or as the god's mount. Small statuettes of *Astarte,* however, have been found in great numbers. These were undoubtedly the small household gods which the Israelitish peasant kept over his hearth. There have also been found many amulets, or luck charms, consisting of blue glass beads or of metal or clay representations of Egyptian gods or beetles, as you may notice in the pictures.

Images of the gods were kept in the home or worn on the person because of the belief that wherever the image was, there the god was present to listen to prayer addressed to him. The more intelligent idol-worshippers understood that the image represented only the likeness or picture of the god. All, however, believed the image possessed of magic qualities, powerful especially in keeping evil spirits from the house. It required many years, therefore, completely to overcome the worship of idols in Israel.

Gods Not Moral

Peasant *Baal* worship differed, furthermore, from the worship of the God of Moses in that the god was not thought of as moral, demanding that persons act righteously. The god's mind might be changed by magic. The mutterings of the magician, a religious dance or the burning of some substance might influence the *Baal* to act as the worshipper desired. The *Baal* was an irresponsible tyrant who desired gifts and answered the prayer of those who brought the largest offerings. Not only the choicest cattle, but even children were occasionally sacrificed. At the

JARS FOR CHILDREN'S BODIES

These jars, with remains of bodies of little infants a few days old, have been found buried under Canaanite high places. These were most likely sacrifices which, while not frequent, were nevertheless the custom. The Hebrew religion fought the practice.

celebrations in honor of the *Baal* the worshippers would drink much wine and, dancing wildly, they would work themselves up into madness, imagining that thereby the spirit of their god would enter into them. They would cut their flesh and shave their heads to attract the attention of their god to them.

HEAD OF A DEMON

This head was of a demon or evil spirit found at Jericho.

Religion Resembles Beliefs of Nomads

Besides the god, spirits, too, were feared and worshipped, especially the spirits of the dead. Sacrifices were offered to the dead as to the gods, and magic was practiced to keep the dead from doing harm. A special group of magicians was believed able to bring the dead up from their graves and to foretell the future. You may recall the story in the Bible about Saul and the witch of Endor.

You may thus recognize the religion of the more

ignorant Israelitish peasant as closely resembling that of his forefathers preceding the time of Moses. Many worshipped *Baal* alone. Others, perhaps the greater number, worshipped both *Baal* and *Y*, considering the former as the god of agriculture and the latter probably as the God of War. In the names of the time, in which it was common to include the name of the gods, many names end with Baal, as for example, Ish Baal, Yerubaal or Meribaal. We even find a name Yabaal, meaning *Y* is *Baal,* showing that the worshipper considered the two religions identical. It is not difficult to understand the confusion, for the Israelites took over the Canaanite sacred high places with all their furnishings and continued their worship there. Today, too, one religious organization frequently buys the buildings of another and continues to use them for its worship.

Lowers Morals of Worshippers

The effect of such religion upon the believers can readily be imagined. A worshipper can be no better than his god. If his god helps only those who offer him gifts and behaves as he pleases without reason, why should man be better? The king and the nobles might, therefore, be tyrannical, extending favor only to those who approach them with gifts. The poor man is thus not only despised by the rich, but even God does not care for him. In Babylon all the re-

ligion and magic were carried on for the benefit of
the king. In Egypt the priests were in the service of
the wealthy nobles, to supply them with what food
and drink they would need in the world to come.
At law, too, a noble was worth more than a poor
man, so that for the killing of the former you might
lose your life, while for the murder of the latter
there was generally only a money penalty.

UPPER LAYER DEVELOPS MOSAIC TEACHINGS

The religion of the highest group was a continuation
of the finer elements of the teachings of Moses. Y
to these believers was the greatest of gods, who
would not permit the worship of any other power
besides himself. The worship of Y was to be free
of magical ideas, that is, of belief that God can be
compelled to do whatever the worshipper desires
through the use of some force over God. Instead, the
worship of Y had to be founded mainly on righteousness and obedience to the law of God. Thus Samuel,
reproving Saul, says:
"Hath the Lord as great delight in burnt-offerings
    and sacrifices,
 As in hearkening to the voice of the Lord?
 Behold, to obey is better than sacrifice,
 And to hearken than the fat of rams.
 For rebellion is as the sin of witchcraft."

I Samuel, Chapter XV, Verses 22–23.

Insist on Moral Conduct

The true worshippers of Y were the ones responsible for the humane spirit in the law codes which we mentioned before. Y to them was too great to take notice of the human differences in wealth or in social position. Rich or poor, king, noble or common were all to be alike before the law. Justice was to be the guide for both king and judge. Justice was to prevail whether it resulted in benefit to the rich man or to the poor. Judges were strictly forbidden to accept gifts, although bringing gifts to the judge was a very common custom at this time. The judges, moreover, were not the only ones responsible for justice, but all the people had their duties. It was to be the concern of the whole nation to provide for the poor, the widow, the fatherless, and the stranger who, too often, was regarded as less deserving than the native or citizen. The Bible constantly reminds our forefathers that they themselves had been strangers in Egypt and that they must, therefore, act kindly to strangers, for they can understand the feelings of the stranger.[1] Justice becomes the watchword of Israel.

[1] At the time of this writing (1930), a bill is being urged in the United States Congress demanding that all aliens register with the governmental authorities. The underlying thought of the bill is that aliens are dangerous or undesirable persons who must be watched especially. We thus see that in the treatment of aliens we are not yet as civilized as the Bible commanded Israel three thousand years ago.

Forbid Images

The second important difference between the religion of Moses and that of Canaan was that the religion of Moses forbade the making of images of Israel's national God. The making of all images was not yet completely abolished even among the highest groups. There were figures of Cherubim, winged creatures, and of a brazen serpent even in the Temple. Y was not to be pictured in any way. It may be hard for us fully to understand what idol-worship or the worship of images was and why the forbidding of idols was of such importance. We have already seen that the idol of wood or of stone was only a picture of the God. Representing God in a shape familiar to man, however, lessens our reverence, since God is far

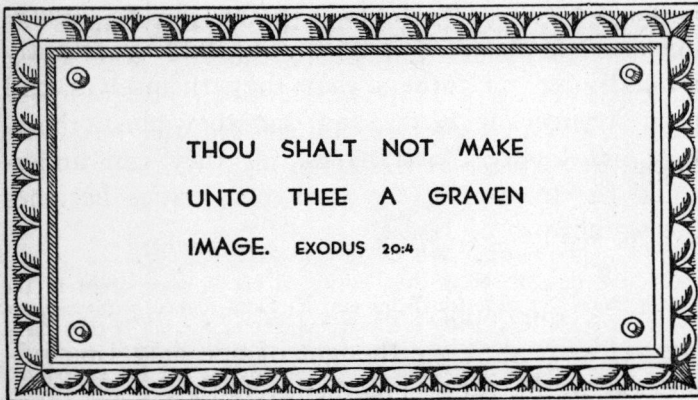

THOU SHALT NOT MAKE UNTO THEE A GRAVEN IMAGE. EXODUS 20:4

greater than anything which can dwell in the body of an animal or of a man. Furthermore, idol worship was harmful because it encouraged the feeling that an idol in the home left the residents free to act as they pleased, relying on their idol for protection.

A third reason why idol worship was a very low form of religion is that it preserved the local petty gods of each place. Each tribe pictures its god in its own way. Should Moses have permitted likenesses to be made of God, each tribe would have represented him in the form of its old god, simply calling the image by the new name. That happened, as we have noted above. Many, too, made their God appear like the *Baalim* of Canaan. The only way to enforce the true religion was to forbid the making of idols, as was done in the second commandment.

The only representation of Israel's God was the Ark of the Covenant, wherein were kept the two tablets of stone. There alone the God of Israel was believed to dwell; and where the Ark was, there he could be especially worshipped. The religious leaders strove, therefore, to give to the Ark particular importance at this time.

Y Rules All Departments of Life

Even the worshippers of the pure "Y" religion had not yet arrived at the thought of one only God ruling the world. They still believed that other gods existed for other peoples, but that the other gods were of lesser importance by comparison with their God Y. There was no need of particular gods for special tasks, such as gods for war, for fertility or for music and other arts. To the Hebrews Y was the god presiding over every department of their life. Yet it remained for the prophetic movement of the following centuries to deny the existence of any other gods in the world except Y, God of Israel.

In similar manner the true worship of Y was opposed to the fear of spirits and to the worship of the dead. Every custom reminding the people of spirits or of worship of the dead was either forbidden or else given different meaning. Thus witchcraft and summoning up the dead were prohibited, as were also the cutting of one's flesh, the shaving of the head or offering gifts of food to the deceased. Pillars formerly set up over departed persons for worship as at a high place now merely became memorial stones.

PRIESTS OF LOWER LAYER

Corresponding with differences in worship, each religious group had its own priests. The Israelites who accepted Canaanitish worship also imitated the Canaanite priesthood, often taking over a high place with all the priests already there. These priests declared themselves to be magicians, medicine men, readers of the heavens or conversers with the dead,

AN ANCIENT ALTAR

The altar, as you see, is a large natural rock. Notice the channels cut all around it to carry away the blood of the sacrificial victims. This altar seems to be in a clearing high up in the mountains.

who knew charms against ghosts and evil spirits. They offered food and drink to the gods, and interpreted the will of the gods to those who asked for it.

The whole lower Canaanite worship was built on superstition, and often even on the inventions of persons who were mentally unbalanced. They asserted that they saw dreams and visions which were accepted as the expression of the will of the gods or as the true appearance of the gods. Here someone reported he had seen a ghost; there someone announced he had heard a voice, a sign which proved that God dwelt in that place. Such places thereafter became sacred, and thousands of worshippers flocked to them at fixed holy days to seek the protection of the spirit. Such were the priests of the lowest religious groups.

In addition to the magic priests at the public

high places, there were the domestic priests. The father, as in the earlier days, continued as the recognized religious head of the household. The eldest son, too, frequently occupied this position, because the first-born was looked upon as belonging to God. If the family was wealthy, it might hire the services of a traveling Levite, as is related in the story of Micah and the Danites (Judges, Chapter XVII). The Levites looked after the needs of the household gods, provided them with food and drink offerings, and burned incense before them. They also offered up the sacrifice at family gatherings and led the family in prayer. In later times they were also teachers of the young.

PRIEST OF MOSAIC FOLLOWERS

The followers of the pure Mosaic religion also worshipped at home and at the high places. The head of the family, the father or the eldest son, offered the sacrifices and may have led the family in prayer. Their ministers at the high places, however, differed from those at the Canaanite shrines. They were generally called Levites, members of the tribe of Levi from which Moses was descended—though whether they actually were the members of that tribe or whether the name "Levite" came to mean a minister of religion is not certain. These priests, besides offering sacrifice, still told people the oracle, by means

SHILOH

The site of the ancient home of Israel's first sanctuary of Y in Canaan.

of the holy lots of which we shall tell presently. Even such a matter as Saul's lost donkeys was the concern of as great a priest as Samuel.[1] Because of their duties of reading the oracle the early priests were also called "seers."

Priests of Principal Shrine Most Important

Since Y was the national God, there generally was one place of worship which was considered the chief or central shrine. Thus we read of the Temple at Shiloh and of the sacred tent in the days of King David. The priests at these centers were regarded as

[1] I Samuel, chap. IX

the leading teachers of the religion of *Y*. We have already noticed the position of importance of such leaders as Eli and Samuel even in matters of war and government. The priests of these sanctuaries, together with the prophets of whom we shall tell later, led the attack against Canaanite worship. One of the very first movements of which we hear among the followers of the Ark of the Covenant was the attempt to drive out the witches and magicians from the land. The movement gained considerable force under Samuel and Saul. Saul had undertaken the task, but was superstitious enough to seek the advice of the witch himself. Samuel, however, and his followers continued explaining to the people what a low idea of God it was to believe that a priest's dancing and muttering could prevent God from doing his will.

The priests of the Ark of the Covenant, in order to fight the magic priests, were obliged not merely to tell people that the magicians were wrong, but also to teach what was right. It was therefore natural for the priests to become the teachers and the judges. "They shall teach Jacob Thine ordinances, and Israel Thy Law,"[1] says the blessing of Moses. Because of the fierce struggle against Canaanitish religion the priests gave much attention to teaching the people and, as a result, education made considerable headway in Israel.

[1] Deuteronomy, chap. XXXIII, v. 10

Other Religious Ministers—Early Prophets Are Magicians

Another group of men whom we might also call ministers of religion were the prophets. In very early days the prophets and the priest were the same person. Prophets were believed to be persons who had dreams or visions sent them by the gods or spirits. These men interpreted their ordinary dreams to be a sign from God, and thus became known as persons who speak with God. Many, therefore, came to them to learn the will of the gods in matters that concerned them. The prophet or priest, as we saw above, gave advice in such a way that he could always claim to be right. If, for example, a person came to ask that his relative be cured from an illness, the prophet might tell him that his relative might be cured if the man and his whole family did nothing to anger the gods. If the sick person died, it was taken as a sign that some member of the family had angered the gods. The word of the prophet was never questioned. People flocked to him, paying him well for his services. Prophecy was a profitable trade.

New Class of Prophets—Moses

Moses, our great lawgiver, was the first of a new class of prophets. We know very little about him ex-

RECENT MAGIC CURES

To this day many persons still hope to be cured through magic. Recently rumor spread that the grave of a priest buried in Malden, Massachusetts, had the power of curing anyone who touched it. The picture shows the throngs of superstitious men and women crowding to get near to the grave.

cept what is bound up in story and legend. We do know, however, as we have seen in an earlier chapter, that he gave Israel a new religion and new idea of God based upon principles of right and wrong. Since God was different from other gods, the prophet, too, had to be different. Moses was honored even by our

earliest ancestors not so much for the miracles which
were told of him as for his moral teachings, for his
laws and judgments. "And there hath not arisen a
prophet since in Israel like unto Moses," says the
Bible, "whom the Lord knew face to face." [1]

After the death of Moses, as we have already told,
the lower classes among the Israelites returned to
their former worship and to the old idol-worshipping
prophets. The faithful followers of Moses, too, had
their prophets; but at this time they could hardly
be distinguished from the Canaanite dervishes.
Known as the "Sons of the Prophets," they went
about dancing, playing and singing, thus arousing
the people. These prophets were active during the
Philistine invasion and helped create a desire among
the various tribes for union in a single monarchy.

Samuel

Soon a higher type of prophet came out of that
group. The eldest prophet of the higher class of
whose work we have any account is Samuel. Samuel
was still called the seer, and people continued to
come to him for the oracle, paying him for his services, as was customary. Samuel was also the chief
priest in charge of the sacrifices and of blessing the
assembly.

However, Samuel was more than a seer: he was

[1] Deuteronomy, chap. XXXIV, v. 10

the teacher of his people, their highest judge and lawmaker. In his old age, when the people were ready for a strong and warlike chief, Samuel was asked to choose the man and to anoint him. More than that, Samuel laid down the laws to govern the king, a constitution which the king must obey. When Saul violated these rules, Samuel reproved him and told him that God was no longer with him. Saul was so greatly in fear of Samuel that he begged him at least to do him honor in the eyes of the people, who otherwise would no longer be obedient to him.

Defenders of Popular Liberties

As the scattered clans in Israel united in one government under a king and as the many local privileges and liberties had to be surrendered to the king, the prophet became the guardian of the rights of the people. Kings of other nations, like their gods, were absolute tyrants. They acted as they pleased; they took of the best for themselves; they decreed life and death to their subjects, and no one could prevent them. The Bible describes the actions of the kings in a famous speech of warning said to have been delivered by Samuel before Saul was chosen king: "He will take your sons, and appoint them unto him, for his chariots, and to be his horsemen; and they shall run before his chariots . . . and to plow his ground, and to reap his harvest, and to make his instruments of war. And he will take your daughters to be perfumers and to be cooks and to be bakers. And he will take your fields, and your vineyards, and your olive-yards, even the best of them——" [1]

Yet Israel had too long been trained in the freedom of the desert to surrender itself to the will of one man. The king of Israel could not reign absolutely as the king of Tyre or Assyria. Whenever he attempted to exercise any tyranny, the fearless prophet was at hand to reprove him in no uncertain language. We have the powerful story of the prophet Nathan before King David. The king had used his power to place one of his captains, Uriah the Hittite, in a dangerous position in battle in order that he, the king, might take unto himself Uriah's wife, Bathsheba. As soon as the report reached the prophet Nathan, he appeared before King David and related the parable of the poor man's ewe lamb which the rich man had stolen. When the king angrily declared the rich man deserving of death, the prophet cried out, "Thou art the man." The king in humble spirit admitted his guilt, fasting and praying for forgiveness. The prophet had established his power as the representative of God and the king respected it.

[1] I Samuel, chap. VIII, vs. 11–12

THOU ART THE MAN
Nathan denounces King David—As the artist imagined it.

Prophets were still asked for oracles, as, for example, whether or not a king should go to war. They
still performed miracles and wonders. The greater
prophets, however, were the forerunners of a new

type of religious teacher who would champion the cause of the common people against oppression by the rulers. In this early period the foundation was laid for the great prophets of the later period, who left us their works in writing, and whose teachings finally educated Israel to cast away the worship of idols and to accept the God of Israel in truth.

ANOTHER TYPE OF HOLY MEN—NAZARITES

There was a special class of holy men who did not occupy any official position among the people. These were known as the Nazarites, men who had taken a vow to be separate or apart from other people. The vow of the Nazarite demanded of him that during the period of his Nazariteship, he should not cut his hair, not drink wines or strong liquors, and not touch anything unholy. A person might be a Nazarite for a number of years or for life. If it was for only a number of years, the end of the Nazarite period was marked with sacrifices, especially with offerings of the hair to God. The whole idea of Nazariteship may have been aimed against the drunken revels of Canaanite life. The Israelite who undertook it was anxious to keep himself especially pure and holy in the spirit of simplicity which recalled nomadic desert life. That a Nazarite was not in all other ways a religious person, as we think of a religious person today, can be gathered from the stories of Samson who, we may remember, was a Nazarite.

WHERE OUR ANCESTORS WORSHIPPED

While there were important differences in religion among various groups, their places of worship resembled each other. Our early ancestors, as we saw, worshipped mostly in the open air, upon the summits of mountains or in forest clearings. When Israel invaded Canaan, it took possession of Canaanitish high places, stone altars and sacred trees, just as it took unto itself Canaanite cities and villages. Every section had its high place, the *Bamah,* where sacrifices were offered, usually to the spirit of the place.

There were a number of cities which were considered particularly sacred. In later times legend went back to the fathers of the Jewish people in order to get reasons for the holiness of these cities. At one place Jacob had had his famous dream; at others Abraham had built altars and called upon the name of God. Such cities as Bethel, Shechem, Beersheba, Hebron and Dan were sacred places where there were either sacred wells or stones or in later days even temples.

The main symbol of the religion of Moses was the Ark of the Covenant. Wherever the Ark of the Covenant was situated, there was the central sanctuary. We recall meeting it at Shiloh for a time; but the disastrous war of the Philistines destroyed Shiloh. For many years there was no substitute city. The Ark had no powerful champion among the people until the rise of King David. In his day the Ark was brought with great honors to the newly established capital. At this period Jerusalem becomes the most famous shrine of Israel; and we shall see the struggle in the years to come to make it the only shrine in the land.

The Furnishings of the Shrine

Most of the shrines, as we have seen, were in the open air. The shrine generally contained an altar of stone or of earth, a flat surface with channels cut around it to carry off the blood. Besides the altar we have already told of the pillar, or in large shrines of the several pillars, and the sacred tree. The shrines of *V* were often also housed in tents, even as late as the days of David. The furnishings within the tent must have been very few and simple. We know that there was a *menorah*, or lamp, burning continuously. There was the table of the show bread, on which were placed the twelve holy loaves in two piles, with a golden dish of fragrant incense above each pile. The breads were always to be present before the Lord. Every Sabbath new bread was baked and the old distributed among the priests, who alone were considered holy enough to eat of the offering.

THE INTERIOR OF THE SHRINE

As imagined by the artist from the description found in the Bible.
Notice particularly the show bread and the Menorah.

The shrine contained an altar and some arrangement
for cooking the meat of the sacrifices. There was
also an *Ephod*, of which we do not have a very exact
notion. In early times the *Ephod* may have been an
idol. Later the word seemed to mean a part of the
priest's dress, somewhat like an apron or a Scotch
kilt. When David came to Nob and asked the priest
for arms, the priest told him that the sword of
Goliath was behind the *Ephod*.

An important part of every sanctuary was the
device for casting lots to decide the oracle. In Israel
it appears to have been called the *Urim* and the
Thummim. These may have been a pair of dice

PROCESSION OF NEBI MOUSA

The Arabs to this day still go on pilgrimages. This picture shows
the Nebi Mousa procession, that is, the procession to a spot which
the Arabs believe to be the grave of the prophet Moses. The Nebi
Mousa festivities occur at the same time of the year as our Passover and may have originated from the same holiday hundreds of
years ago.

which were cast before the *Ephod,* one being taken
to mean "yes" and the other "no."

FEASTS AND FASTS

Israel in its nomadic state undoubtedly had its festivals when it settled in Canaan. Festivals, however,
are greatly influenced by the occupations of a peo-

ple. Nomadic celebrations represent shepherd life. Israel in Canaan now began to accept agricultural holidays.

There may have been many festivals of local *Baalim* or of various high places of which we no longer have any record. To this day the Arabic peasants of Palestine visit some of the ancient high places on certain occasions and offer gifts there. The main festivals which our ancestors observed must have been celebrated by all groups. They represented a combination of old shepherd celebrations together with new holidays learned from the Canaanites or, at any rate, related to the experience of the farmer. In later times new reasons were added, connecting the celebrations with incidents in the exodus from Egypt.

The most important festivals were the Sabbaths and New Moons. Work and business were stopped on these days and family sacrifices were offered. It appears to have been the custom to visit the priest or the prophet on those days in the same way as we at the present time visit the synagogue.

The Three Festivals

The three main feasts, Passover, Shabuoth and Sukkoth were the festivals of all farmer peoples. *Passover,* also celebrated by nomads with the offering of first-born lambs, began the season of the barley harvest, followed seven weeks later by *Shabuoth*, the time of the ripening of wheat. *Sukkoth* in the fall was the season of the final ingathering of the grapes and of the olives. These festivals, it seems, began with a fast-day and ended in feasting, sacrifice, dancing, general merry-making, and rejoicing before the Lord. The custom early grew up for the men, or in many cases for the whole family, to make a pilgrimage to the main shrine. Thus Elkanah, the father of Samuel, visited Shiloh every year. Later the law commanded that all males come before the Lord at each of the three festivals; and they were not permitted to come empty-handed. On Passover they brought an *omer* of fresh barley, on Shabuoth a basket of the first ripe fruits, and on Sukkoth the tithes (a tenth of their crop) for priest and Levite.

Rosh Hashanah, the celebration of the New Year, may already have been observed, though most likely not in the order in which it appears at present. *Yom Kippur* was probably not yet instituted.

In this connection we might also mention the Sabbatical year, which occurred every seventh year. During that year fields were to lie fallow, and whatever grew of itself was free to be taken by the poor.

Local Holidays

In addition to the religious festivals there were other occasions for rejoicing. The time for the sheep-shearing was a period of festivity and merrymaking. The day of the return of victorious armies and the division of the booty was a great holiday. Special local holidays were also common, such as the four day remembrance of Jephtha's daughter. The king might order a legal holiday, a day of feasting or of mourning, as the occasion demanded. Fasts were occasionally ordered in time of great calamity, in war, or when the rains failed. Thus David prayed and fasted when his child was ill. Saul ordered a fast day till the enemy should be beaten. We find many similar examples in the Bible.

Methods of Worship and Festivity

The oldest methods of worship were offerings or gifts to God which, we today call sacrifices. Sacrifices might be of flour, wine, oil or animals. The person offering the sacrifice prepared himself by washing and changing his garments. In the case of animal sacrifices the animal was killed either on· or near the altar and its blood caught and sprinkled over the altar. Then a portion was burned for the God and the rest was generally eaten by the worshipper in a common meal with God. The sacrifice was usually accompanied by singing, religious dances, games and competitions, as is still common among peoples in early stages of civilization.

The earliest prayers were probably charms by

ARAB DANCES

Dancing is a usual feature of religious celebrations among Arabs today. The dances are for men only. Often these are continued for days, the men working themselves into a frenzy till they fall down exhausted.

which the magicians thought they could bring good luck or drive away evil spirits. The worshippers who brought an offering would often accompany the prayer with a request of some sort from the God. As the higher religion of Moses began to spread and people began to lose faith in the mumbling magicians, new and finer prayers began to appear, possibly in the form of hymns. A beautiful example of such a hymn is the song of Hannah found in the Book of Samuel.[1]

[1] Samuel I, chap. II

THE RELIGION OF THE AVERAGE ISRAELITE— A SUMMARY

The religion of the average Israelite was a mixture of local *Baal*-worship with the fear of his own God. He had great reverence and fear for the God who had brought him out of the land of Egypt. Three times yearly he came before the Lord and brought his gifts to the Levite and priest. He feared the prophets of his God and hearkened to them.

However, the Israelite did not yet comprehend a

GAMES

Games and races, too, are still common. The picture shows an Arab high jumping. His costume is not exactly our notion of athletic outfit.

God who was everywhere. God dwelt in Zion, many miles away from his home. Much nearer, in his very hearth, were the household spirits, perhaps the spirits of his departed ancestors, who might do him harm if he did not satisfy them. On the mountains or at the well lived the *Baal* of the Canaanites, the god who was conquered and was, therefore, less important than his chief God, but still a god to be feared and respected.

The average Israelite was still afraid to be without the protection of the *Teraphim*.[1] Israel was learning the new religion, but it learned very slowly, and all the while it clung to its old gods. Many hundreds of years were yet to pass before Israel would discover that there was but one God who lived, not on a mountain top or even in the heavens, but in the mind and in the heart of man.

CULTURAL PROGRESS—AN ADVANTAGE

Cultural progress means progress in knowledge, in books and literature, in music, painting, sculpture and the like. How far did our ancestors advance in these branches, and were such advances entirely of benefit? We shall see that our ancestors did make progress in these fields; and, while such advance was as yet small, whatever it was spelled improvement.

[1] Teraphim were idols, probably household gods.

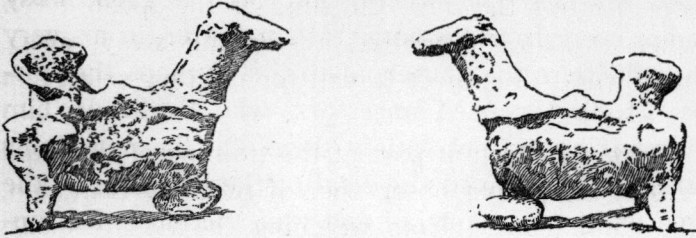

TOYS FOR ISRAELITE CHILDREN

These little animals were toys made of clay. A hole was drilled through one of the legs through which a string was tied for pulling the animal.

Education of the Children

Boys and girls will be interested to learn that in these early days there were no schools. Most children learned by watching their elders perform their work. The wealthier families engaged nurses, male and female, or Levites, who taught their children.

The most important study for every child was that of learning an occupation. The boys learned from their fathers and the girls from their mothers. It was the custom for boys to follow the occupation of their fathers, so that we find a certain trade carried on by the same family for many generations. Even such professions as the priesthood, that of the seer or the musician were usually handed over from father to son.

Another branch of training which every boy had to pass through was practice in using weapons of

war, such as the bow, the sling or the spear. Even
when the king organized a standing army, every
male was still subject to call for military service in
time of war.

A very important part of the training of the child
was in the proper observance of religion. That, too,
the child learned from watching the religious customs of the home or from visiting the sanctuary
with his elders. The studies which boys and girls
have today were hardly known. Only the very
learned men knew how to read or write; but this
knowledge was beginning to spread, especially in the
priesthood and the upper classes.

Literature

The nomadic Israelites, like all other early peoples,
doubtless did not know how to read or write and,
therefore, possessed no books. They did have literature, however, consisting of stories, songs, poems,
riddles and wise sayings, all handed down orally by
priests, bards, prophets and often by the fathers and
mothers.

After the settlement, when the Israelites learned
to write, many of these stories were written down,
as were new books, poems and songs. The Bible mentions some of these early books: *"Sefer Hayashar"*
(The Book of the Upright) or *"Sefer Milhamoth
Adonoi"* (The Book of the Wars of the Lord), which

HEBREW MUSICIANS

This picture from an Assyrian monument shows Hebrew captives playing their lyres.

however, were lost. Many of the beautiful poems found in the Bible, such as David's Lament over Saul (II Samuel, Chapter I, 19–27) or the Song of the Well (Numbers, Chapter XXI 17–20) are taken from these old books. The Song of Deborah (Judges, Chapter V) and the Blessings of Jacob (Genesis, Chapter XLIX) and Moses (Deuteronomy, Chapter XXXIII) also may already have been written at this time.

Music, Painting and Sculpture

We learn from the Bible that our ancestors were very fond of music. King David was as famous for his harp as for his deeds of valor. Many musical instruments are mentioned, such as the harp, the viol, the flute, the trumpet, drums and cymbals. There were also choruses of singers, men as well as women, at festivals and other gatherings.

In sculpture and in painting Israel took very little part. The making of pictures or images was forbidden by law and was, therefore, hardly encouraged.

In skilled handwork and in architecture Israel was beginning to learn from their neighbors, the more expert Canaanites, and especially from the Phoenicians. At this time very little had as yet been accomplished in those fields.

WAR—GAIN AND LOSS

Fighting is the chief business of nomads. They are always at war with everybody. "His hand shall be against every man, and every man's hand against him,"[1] says the Bible of Ishmael. To the desert nomad the law of might is the highest law.

How did settled life change this condition? The effect of settled life on war was in two different directions. It made for more peace and for more war. It made war less frequent, but it also made it more serious.[2] The cost of waging war became greater and war, therefore, became rarer; but to engage in war was now far more dangerous than it had been because of the development of newer weapons.

Longer Periods of Peace but Wars More Serious

Settled peoples cannot always be engaged in warfare. Agriculture and commerce prosper in time of

---

[1] Genesis, chap. XVI, v. 12.
[2] As we have advanced in civilization, our wars have become only slightly less frequent, but much more dangerous.

peace, not in time of war. Accordingly, we read in the Bible that after a serious war the land was at peace for twenty or forty years.

It was a new and strange experience to pass so many years without fighting, and the people were the happier for it. The idea was taking root that human beings were happier when they lived at peace with one another.

Yet only the smallest beginning of the desire for peace was evident. War was still the most important and the most honorable work of a man.[1] If there was peace for a time, that period was employed by the military leaders to prepare more thoroughly for the next war.

War no longer took the form of a raid upon the enemy, to be followed by the quick retreat of the attacking party. War was the business of the heads of the people. The king was chosen because he was the best fighter. The brave men and able generals were made noblemen. Many chose to make fighting their only occupation, and were formed into a standing army.

Up to this time at the close of a war all soldiers returned to their tents and flocks. Now there were some men who were either engaged in making war upon somebody or else went about idle until another war had to be fought.

---

[1] Such a condition existed in Europe till modern times. In some countries it is still true.

Nobility Profits Through War

As it was to the interest of the farmer and the hand-worker to have peace, so it was to the interest of the king, his soldiers and his generals to have war. If the war was successful, the king levied taxes or tributes of gold upon the conquered people. This he did in order to fill his treasury as well as the coffers of his generals. If he conquered a country, he appointed his generals as governors and his soldiers were given the best fields and houses of the enemy. The conquered enemy was enslaved and made to do the work of the conqueror. Instead of a raid for camels or for sheep, war now became a raid for lands, for gold and silver, and for human slaves.

Since the kings of other nations also had their soldiers and noblemen, and since they were also anxious to enrich themselves at the expense of their neighbors, the opportunities for war were many. Wars were undertaken either for offense or for defense. Israel's struggle for union represents first a long war of offense against the inhabitants of Canaan, then of defense against invaders. After Saul had warred defensively against the Philistines, he undertook offensive war against Amalek. David carried the war of offense further than any other king of Israel. He conquered his neighbors on the east and south, from Damascus to the Gulf of Elah.

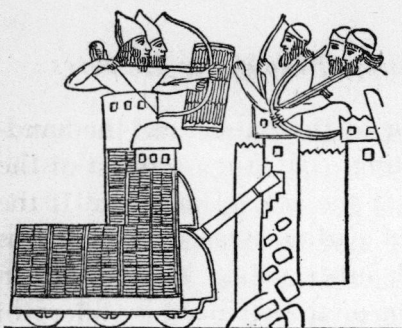

ANCIENT WAR ENGINE

This picture shows an Assyrian battering ram. The ram was a long, heavy pole often as long as 100 feet, tipped at one end with iron, generally shaped like a ram's head. The pole is hung from another pole above it. Soldiers swing the ram against the city walls in order to break them down. To protect the soldiers, a shed was built as part of the engine, and the entire machine was placed on wheels so that it could be moved about easily.

These were serious wars. Often they were long and bitter struggles. For such encounters men had to be well trained. The equipment had to be better. The rude and simple weapons of nomads now gave way to more deadly ones. Iron was now used for swords and arrowheads. Slingers became so expert that they could hit a mark and not miss by a hair's breadth.

In time we shall see how chariots and horses were employed in warfare. The enemy too, had such weapons at their disposal. Cities had to be stormed and walls scaled. For such fighting special machinery was needed. Better weapons naturally killed more people on both sides. In addition, the soldiers were better trained. Their leaders always encouraged them to fight for the glory and honor of their country, and thousands of brave young men willingly gave their lives on the battlefields.

Small Size of Countries Encourages Disputes

The step from the clan to the nation had removed
many causes for fighting; but the step was still
small. Peace was not yet the goal of any great part
of the people. If at an earlier stage Israel shared
part of the desert with other tribes, it now shared
a much smaller fraction of the civilized world with
other settled nations. We can easily understand why
there were such frequent opportunities for quarrels
in the ancient world when we look at the checkerboard map, at the many petty nations, each one certain that it was the bravest, wisest and best, each
one having its own god, for whose honor it would
fight anybody anywhere. In the further study of the
history of our people we shall see that Israel learned
to think of its God as the God of more and more
peoples. When in time it recognized that one God
rules the whole world, it began to hope for greater
and more lasting peace.

SUMMARY

There have now passed before us in review the
changes which Israel underwent when it became a
settled people in Canaan. Did Israel benefit from
these changes? We must answer without hesitation
that it did. It is true that some of the advantages

brought evils in their train. New economic conditions created division among social classes and encouraged magical rites in religion. Cities gave greater protection, but also made war more deadly. However, summing up all the changes, we can readily see how greatly our ancestors were the gainers.

We need only return to the earlier pages to see what great progress had been made over the former days. Now Israel did have cities, fields and houses. Life was much safer, and food and water were more certain. Men learned many new occupations, skills and art. They learned new and valuable ideas in law and religion. If superstitions still persisted, magic and magicians were beginning to lose their hold upon the people. Ideas of right and wrong grew finer. Israel met more strangers and learned to look upon them in a more humane way. Such changes take hundreds of years to accomplish. Our nation was still young, but not as young as it was when we first met it. Israel still had far to ascend on the ladder of progress; but it had climbed considerably since its earliest beginnings.

The story thus far has told of the youth of our people. We have observed our people's beginnings, its organization into a united nation, its settlement of a land and its learning the essential skills of settled life. Israel is now already a grown nation, ready to take its place in the family of nations. What position was Israel able to maintain in its world? Did it hold a place of dignity and honor? How long was it able to retain its safety and independence? Did it prove to be outstanding or distinguished in any way? Did it achieve anything of worth which is deserving of remembrance by later generations? The answers to these questions will form the theme of a succeeding volume.

SUPPLEMENTARY WORK

SUPPLEMENTARY WORK

SUGGESTIONS FOR BIBLE STUDY

Section six has told about many interesting facts in the life of our early ancestors. You might like to know what the Bible has to say about some of these questions. We have listed for you here references to some sections of the Bible which will help you to understand more fully any matter in which you are interested.

ADVANTAGES OF SETTLED LIFE

Deuteronomy VI, 10–15, VIII, 1–18. See how in the first passage the Bible warns Israel against following the religion of the people in whose midst they are settled. The second passage compares the hardship of the desert with the comfort of settled life.

What the wife of a wealthy Hebrew farmer and cattle raiser sent as a gift to David is told in I Samuel XXV, 18, and *Into the Promised Land*, pp. 90–91.

NEW OCCUPATIONS

Some of the new occupations which were developing may be judged from the chapter in which Samuel warns the people of the tasks for which the king would employ their sons and daughters. It is not certain that Samuel did really say these words, but this must have been written at about the time of which we are telling. I Samuel VIII, 11–18, and *Into the Promised Land*, p. 58.

335

II Samuel V, 11, shows that skilled workmen still had to be brought from other countries. See also *Into the Promised Land,* p. 105.

THE CITY

Note what this story tells about the gates, the market place and the judges. Lot still wishes to continue the nomadic hospitality but see how the citizens of Sodom regard the strangers. Genesis XIX, 1–16, and the *Story of Genesis,* pp. 37–38.

The Gate is closed at night, Joshua II, 5, and *Into the Promised Land,* p. 3.

The well is at the market place outside of the city. Genesis XXIV, 10 ff., and the *Story of Genesis,* p. 52.

Strangers sleep in the market place, unless someone takes them into the house. Judges XIX, 10–21.

HOME AND FURNISHINGS

A home is furnished for David on his flight, II Samuel XVII, 27–28, and *Into the Promised Land,* p. 129.

What the roof chamber was used for and how it was furnished is told in II Kings IV, 10, and Jacob D. Schwarz, *In the Land of Kings and Prophets,* pp. 65–66. (This story belongs to a somewhat later period.)

The law about building roofs shows the use to which the roof was put. Deuteronomy XXII, 8, and *Into the Promised Land,* p. 154.

BLOOD RELATIONSHIP GIVES PLACE TO NATIONAL PATRIOTISM
Rise of Social Classes

Saul goes to rescue of Jabesh-Gilead, I Samuel XI and *Into the Promised Land,* pp. 58–61.

But the clan is still important in the life of its members as shown by David's going home for a family sacrifice and considering it important enough to be excused from court. I Samuel XX, 5–6, and *Into the Promised Land,* p. 79.

(Poor and provisions for them will be given under Laws.)

Hard times cause people to turn outlaws, I Samuel XXII, 2, and *Into the Promised Land,* p. 84.

The king can award special privilege, I Samuel XVII, 25.

The king can give away fields and vineyards, I Samuel XXII, 7, and *Into the Promised Land,* p. 84.

Law and Justice

The famous code of Laws which is called the Book of the Covenant contains all the laws discussed in this section. Read the following chapters: Exodus XXI to XXIII, 19, and *Out of the House of Bondage,* pp. 66–68.

Religion

Israel worships Baal—Judges II, 11–13.

A good picture of early religion is found in the story of Micah and the Danites, Judges XVII and XVIII.

Another famous story showing the religion of the lower elements is that of the Golden Calf, Exodus XXXII, 1–14, and *Out of the House of Bondage,* pp. 70–72.

A famous story protesting against child sacrifice is the Sacrifice of Isaac, Genesis XXII, and the *Story of Genesis,* pp. 44–47.

There are numerous references to images and household gods used for worship, I Samuel XIX, 11–17, particularly verse 13, tells of teraphim that look like persons. The story of the Golden Calf has already been mentioned.

Gideon makes an ephod, Judges VIII, 22–28, particularly verse 27. (We do not know what this ephod was like.)

Religion of Upper Layer

Samuel's farewell address shows how the true worship of Y prized upright conduct, I Samuel XII.

Nathan denounced David, II Samuel XII, 1–15 or *Into the Promised Land*, pp. 113–117.

How worship was carried on at Shiloh is described in I Samuel I–III, and *Into the Promised Land*, pp. 48–54.

The laws also show the spirit of the religion in perhaps the finest way. Reread the laws already referred to.

Images are forbidden in the second commandment, Exodus XX, 3–5, and *Out of the House of Bondage*, p. 64.

Early Priests and Prophets

Samuel tells Saul he will meet a company of "Sons of Prophets," I Samuel X, 1–11.

The prophet of old is called Seer. Note also what the seer was believed able to do. I Samuel IX.

The early Levites were wandering priests. Read about the Levite in story of Micah and Danites, Judges XVII and XVIII.

Later Levites are believed to be only the true ministers of Y. They battle for the Lord at the end of the story of Golden Calf, Exodus XXXII, 26–35.

Levites are described as ministers and teachers in the song of Moses, Deuteronomy XXXIII, 8–11.

Oracles and Casting of Lots

David consults the oracle, I Samuel XXIII, 1–4.

Joshua casts lots to discover the guilty persons, Joshua VII.

Saul consults the oracle and casts lots to find the cause of God's anger, I Samuel XIV, 36–45.

Nazarites

The laws governing the Nazarite are found in Numbers VI, 1–21.

Samson becomes a Nazarite, Judges XIII, and *Into the Promised Land*, p. 35.

Where Our Ancestors Worshipped

Sacrifices were brought on Mount Carmel—I Kings XVIII, 19–39, and *In the Land of Kings and Prophets*, pp. 22–25.

The believed origin of holy cities is described in Genesis XII, 6–8, and in the *Story of Genesis*, pp. 24–26.

A sacred tree is mentioned in Genesis XIII, 18.

An angel appears at a sacred well, Genesis XVI, 7–14.

The sacred stone or Mazebah is referred to in Genesis XXVIII, 10–22, and in the *Story of Genesis*, pp. 71–73.

Furnishing of the Central Shrine

The story of desert tabernacle may describe how the inside of a shrine was furnished, Exodus Ch. XL, 1–33.

THE FESTIVALS
The Sabbath

See the fourth commandment, Exodus XX, 8–12, and *Out of the House of Bondage*, pp. 64–65.

God rested on seventh day, Genesis II, 1–3, *Story of Genesis*, p. 4, and Exodus XXXI, 12–17.

The three festivals are commanded in Exodus XXIII, 14–17 and again in Exodus XXXIV, 21–24.

The festival of seventh month is mentioned in I Kings VIII, 2, and *Into the Promised Land*, p. 157. (Notice that the name of month is different from what we call it today and the festival seems different also.)

New Moons

David fears he will be missed at New Moons celebration, I Samuel XX, 5 ff., and *Into the Promised Land*, p. 79.

Private Festivals

Sheep shearing was an occasion for rejoicing, II Samuel XIII, 23 ff.

At special occasions dances were held in the vineyards at Shiloh, Judges XXI, 19–24.

The lament over Jephtha's daughter became a regular festival, Judges XI, 39–40, and *Into the Promised Land*, p. 34.

METHOD OF WORSHIP

Reread the story of the Golden Calf, Exodus XXXII, particularly 6, and *Out of the House of Bondage*, pp. 69–74.

Reread the first chapter of I Samuel.

Reread Jacob's dream, Genesis XXVIII, 10–22, particularly 18–19, and the *Story of Genesis*, pp. 71–73. Moses offers a sacrifice in Exodus XXIV, 4–11.

EARLY LITERATURE

The references are given in the text.

MUSIC

Note the instruments carried by the prophets whom Saul meets, I Samuel X, 5.

Singing men and singing women are mentioned in II Samuel XIX, 36.

PAINTING AND SCULPTURE FORBIDDEN

Reread the second Commandment, Exodus XX, 3–5, and *Out of the House of Bondage*, 64. See also Deuteronomy Ch. IV, 14–19, and *Out of the House of Bondage*, pp. 146–147.

WAR

A standing army is raised by Saul, I Samuel XIV, 52.

David has permanent officers and guard, II Samuel XV, 18, and II Samuel XX, 23.

David introduces chariots, II Samuel VIII, 4.

Cruelty of ancient wars is described in the story of Jabesh-Gilead, I Samuel XI and *Into the Promised Land*, pp. 38–61, also in II Samuel VIII, 1–2, and XII, 31, where it is told how David slays two-thirds of Moabites. Saving the one-third was considered an act of kindness.

QUESTIONS FOR THOUGHT AND DISCUSSION

1. Is it better for people to share all property or to own it privately?
2. The Jewish immigrant who has come to America has certainly learned many valuable lessons in his new American home. Has he also learned some lessons that are not fine? What has the immigrant learned that is good and what that is not?
3. Is it better for life to change or always to remain the same? Should some things change and others not? Which?
4. Is a variety of occupations beneficial?
5. Why are there few Jewish farmers today? Would the condition of the Jews be better if there were more Jewish farmers throughout the world?

6. Why were ancient or medieval cities so much smaller than cities today?

7. Are richer nations generally more advanced in civilization than poorer peoples? Give proofs for or against either side.

8. Should we always take the part of our brother, club member or friend whether he is right or wrong? Answer honestly what you would really do if your friend was engaged in a quarrel or argument. State your reasons.

9. Should we always take the side of our country even when it is wrong? Give examples.

10. Whose fault is it that some people are poor? What ought we to do about poverty?

11. How should our justice be made more just?

12. How and how well do we provide for the poor, the widow and the orphan today?

13. Do all persons who are supposedly of one denomination share common beliefs or do we have upper and lower layers within the same religious groups today?

14. Are there any changes going on in religion today? Are these changes for the better or not? Give examples.

15. Is it a good thing to have large, costly and beautiful synagogues or would we pray better in humble rooms or out of doors as people used to thousands of years ago?

16. How have methods of worship changed? Is our manner of worship as good as can be or can it still be improved? How?

17. Is warfare more humane today than it was in ancient times?

ADDITIONAL READINGS

FOR PUPILS

Hunting, *op. cit.*, pp. 39–65.

Spivak, M. J., "Romance and Tragedy in Arabia"—The Story of the Jews of Yemen, *The Young Judaean*, Vol. XVI, October, 1926, pp. 6 ff.

This story tells of Jews living in Yemen, southern Arabia, amidst the Arabs today whose civilization is much like that of our ancestors of the time of Saul and David.

Furth, Jesse C., "Up to Zion's Hill." A tale of pilgrimage in Bible Days. *The Young Judaean*, Vol. XVI, May, 1926, pp. 2 f.

Golub, Rose, "A Visit to the Samaritans," *Young Israel*, Vol. XXII, April, 1930, pp. 8–10.

The Samaritans are an arab people living on the site of ancient Shechem. Their manner of celebrating the Passover still resembles the way in which our ancestors of old observed the holiday.

FOR TEACHERS

McCurdy, *op. cit.*, Vol. II, chaps. IV, V, VI, as much as applies to this section. The same references will also be used for section IX in Vol. II.

Noyes, *op. cit.*, pp. 188–211.

Radin, Max, *The Life of People in Biblical Times*. Philadelphia, The Jewish Publication Society of America, 1929.

Bertholet, *op. cit.*, pp. 148 to end. Same reference will also be given for section IX in Vol. II.

Pronouncing List

ā—pāy; ă—băd; ä—ärt; ē—mē; ĕ—bĕd; ē̃—fē̃rn;
ī—īce; ĭ—tĭn; ō—gō; ŏ—nŏt; ū—rūle; ŭ—rŭn.

Abiathar—ăb-ī'ăth-är
Abimelech—a-bĭm'i-lĕk
Abinoam—ă-bĭn'ŏ-ăm
Abiram—ă-bī'răm
Abner—ăb'nēr
Abraham—ā'bra-hăm
Absalom—ăb'săl-ŏm
Achish—ā'kĭsh
Adonis—a-dō'nĭs
Amalek—ăm'ăl-ĕk
Amalekite—ăm-ăl'ĕk-īt
Ammon—ăm'mŏn
Ammonite—ăm'mŏn-īt
Arab—ăr'ab
Arabia—ă-rā'bĭ-ă
Arabian Desert—ă-rā'bĭ-an
Aram-Naharaim—ā-răm nä-
  hä-rä'-ĭm
Aramean—är"ăm-ē'ăn
Arnon—är'non
Ashdod—ăsh'dŏd
Asher—ăsh'ēr
Asherah (sacred tree)—ă-shē'-
  räh
Ashkelon—ăsh'kĕl-ŏn
Ashtaroth (Astarte) ăsh'to-
  rĕth
Asia—ā'she
Astarte—ăs-tär'tē
Assyria—ăs-sĭr'ĭ-ă
Assyrians—ăs-sĭr'ĭ-ăn
Baal—bā'ăl
Baalim—bā'ă-lĭm

Babylon—băb'y-lŏn
Babylonians—băb'y-lō-nĭ-an
Balaam—bā'lăm
Balak—bā'lăk
Barah—bā'răk
Beersheba—bē"ĕr-shē'bă
Benjamin—bĕn'jă-mĭn
Benjamites—bĕn'jăm-ītes
Beth Shemesh—bĕth-shĕm'-
  ĕsh
Bethel—bĕth'ĕl
Bible—bī'bl
Canaan—kā-năn
Canaanites—kā'nan-ītes
Cherubim—chĕr'ŭ-bĭm
Chaldea—kăl-dē'ă
Chinnereth—kĭn'ĕ-rŏth
Crete—crēt
Dagon—dā-gŏn
Damascus—dă-măs'cŭs
Dan—dăn
Danites—dăn'ītes
David—dā'vĭd
Deborah—dĕb'ŏ-räh
Deuteronomy—dyū"ter-ŏn'-
  o-mī
Dothan—dō'thăn
Eben-ezer—ĕb"ĕn-ēz'ĕr
Edom—ē'dŏm
Egypt—ē'jĭpt
Egyptians—ē-jĭp'shŭn
Ekron—ĕk'rŏn
Elah—ē'läh

344

Eldad and Medad—ĕl′dăd: mē-dăd
Eleazer of Damascus —ĕl-ē-ā′zär
Elkanah—ĕl-kā-näh
Eli—é-lī
Ephod—ĕ′fŏd
Ephraim—ē′frĭ-ĭm
Ephraimite—ē-fră-ĭm-īt
Eretz Yisroel—ĕ″rĕtz-yis rō-ĕl′
Esau—ē′sa
Esdraelon—ĕs″dra-ē′lon
Exodus—ĕks′ō-dŭs
Fellahin—fĕl″löh-een′
Galilee—găl′i-lē
Gath—găth
Gaza—gā′ză
Gera—ge′ră
Genesis—gĕn′e-sĭs
Gezer—gē′zer
Gibeonites—gĭb′ĕ-ŏn-īts
Gideon—gĭd′e-on
Gilboa—gĭl-bō′ă
Gilead—gĭl′ĕ-ăd
God—gôd
Goliath—gō-lī-ăth
Goshen—gō′shĕn
Hammurabi—hä-mu-rä′bï
Hannah—hăn′näh
Hebrew—hē-brū
Hebron—hĕb′rŏn
Hiram—hī′răm
Hittite—hĭt′īt
Hofni—hŏf′nĭ
Isaac—ī′sac
Isaachar—ĭs′a-cär
Ish Baal—ĭsh-bā′al
Ishmael—ĭsh′mă-ĕl
Ish Bosheth—ĭsh-bō′shĕth

Israel—ĭz′ră-ĕl
Jabesh - Gilead — jā″bĕsh-gĭl′-ĕ-ăd
Jabbok—yā′bok
Jacob—jā′kŏb
Jebusite—jĕb′yū-sīt
Jephtha's daughter—jĕf′thäh
Jericho—jĕr′ĭ-kō
Jerusalem—jĕ-rū′să-lĕm
Jesse—jes′i
Jethro—jĕth′rō
Jezreel—jĕz′rĕ-ĕl
Jonathan—jŏn′ă-thăn
Jordan—jōr′dăn
Joshua—jŏsh′yū-ŭh
Judaeans—jū-dē′ans
Judah—jū′däh
Kadesh Barnea—kă-dĕsh
"Kein Ayin Orah"—kān″ī-yĭn-hŏ′rä
Kenites—kē′nīt
Kenizzites—kē-nĕz′īts
Kish—kĭsh
Kishon—kĭsh′ŏn
Korah—kō-räh
Levite—lē′vīt
Lex Talionis—lĕks tăl′i-ŏn-ĕs
Lot—lŏt
Mahanaim—mā″ha-nā′im
Mazebah (pillar)—ma-tzeh′-va
Mediterranean Sea—mĕd″i-tĕ-rā′ne-an
Megiddo—mĕ-gĭd′dō
Menasseh—mă-năs′sĕ
Menorah—mĕ-nō′ra
Mesopotamia—mĕs″o-po-tā′-mi-a
Michael Angelo—mī-kel-ān′-jē-lō

Midian—mĭd′ĭ-ăn
Midianites—mĭd′ĭ-ăn-īts
Moab—mō′ăb
Mosaic Teachings—mo-sā′ic
Moses—mō′zĕz
Mount Carmel—kär′mĕl
Mount Gilboa—gĭl-bō′ă
Mount Herman—hĕr′man
Mount Horeb—hō′rĕb
Mount Zion—zī′ŏn
Mountains of Ephraim—
    ē′fră-ĭm
Mountains of Judah—jū′däh
Naphtali—năf′tă-lī
Nathan—nā′thăn
Nazarites—năz′ĭ-rīt
Nile—nīl
Omer—ō′mĕr
Ophra—ŏf′räh
Paran—pā′răn
Patriarch—pā′tri-ärc
Pharaoh—fā′rō
Philistia—fĭ-lĭs′ti-a
Philistines—fĭ-lĭs′tĭns
Phineas—fĭn′e-hăs
Phoenicia—fe-nĭsh′i-a
Phoenicians—fe-nĭsh′ans
Pithom—pī′thŏm
Ramah—rā′ma
Rameses—răm′e-sēs
Reuben—rū′ben
Rosh Hashanah—rōsh-hä-
    shä′nä
Sabbatical Year—să-băt′i-cal
Samaria—să-mār′ĭ-ă
Samson—säm′son
Samuel—săm′yū-ĕl
Sanctuary—sănk′chū-ĕ-rĭ
Saul—sŏl
Sefer Hayashar—sā-fer-hä-

yă′shăr
Sefer Mulhamoth Adonoi—
    sä″ fer-mŭl-hŏ′moth-ă-dō-
    noy′
Shabuoth—shä′bu-ŏth
Sharon—shăr′on
Sheba ben Bichri—shĕ-ba-
    bĕn-bic″ri
Shechem—shē′kĕm
Shephala—shĕf-ā′loh
Sheter—shĕ′ter
Shew Bread—shō′brĕd
Shiloh—shī′lōh
Simeon—sĭm′ĭ-ŏn
Sinai—sī′nī
Sisera—sĭs′ĕr-ă
Sodom and Gomorrah—sŏ′-
    dŏm & go-mŏr′a
Song of Deborah—dĕb′ŏ-räh
Sukkoth—sūk-ōth
Syrian Desert—sўr′i-an
Taanach—tā′a-năc
Tammuz—tăm-ŭz
Tebulum—tĕ-bū-lom′
Teraphim—tĕr′a-fĭm
Thebez—thē-bĕz
Tora—tō′rä
Tyre—tīr
Uriah the Hittite—yū-rī-äh
Urim & Thumin—yū′rim &
    thŭm′im
Vendetta—vĕn-dĕt′a
Yabaal—yă-bā′al
Yahvneh—yăv-nĕh
Yarmuck River—yăr′muk
Yerubaal—yĕ-rū-bā′al
Yom Kippur—yŏm kĭp′ur
Zebulun—zĕb′ū-lŭn
Ziklag—zĭk′lăg
Zuph—zŭf

Index

347